SONGS AND POEMS OF THE SOUTH.

SONGS AND POEMS

OF

THE SOUTH.

BY A. B. MEEK,

AUTHOR OF

"THE RED EAGLE," "ROMANTIC PASSAGES IN SOUTHWESTERN HISTORY," etc.

FOURTH EDITION.

MOBILE:
S. H. GOETZEL & CO., 33 DAUPHIN STREET.
NEW YORK:—117 FULTON STREET.
1857.

FRENCH & WHEAT,
Printers and Stereotypers
No. 18 Ann Street New York

PREFACE.

THE Poetry of a country should be a faithful expression of its physical and moral characteristics. The imagery, at least, should be drawn from the indigenous objects of the region, and the sentiments be such as naturally arise under the influence of its climate, its institutions, habits of life, and social condition. Verse, so fashioned and colored, is as much the genuine product and growth of a Land, as its trees or flowers. It partakes of the raciness of the soil, the purity of the atmosphere, the brilliancy of its skies, its mountain pictures, and its broad sweeps of level and undulating territory. The Scenery infuses itself into the Song; and the feelings and fancies are modulated by the circumstances amid which they had their birth.

These opinions have formed the poetic Faith of the writer of the present volume. He has not attempted to sing in a mere spirit of imitativeness, or in the tropes and metaphors of foreign Art and Precedent. Gazing upon the delightful Land about him—the Land of his birth and affections—he has endeavored to depict its beauties,—to weave its illustrative objects into the tissues of his imagination, and to give utterance to the thoughts and emotions congenial to a mind impressed by such associations, and loving at once the Patriotic and the Beautiful.

For this reason, the writer has felt warranted in styling the contents of the present volume, "SONGS AND POEMS OF THE SOUTH." If they possess any merit, it is in their fidelity to the principles just declared. But the writer is still well aware of their deficiency, even in that respect. They are but feeble and desultory attempts in the expanded field of his Philosophy,—doing but ill-proportioned justice, even in the simplest aspects, to either the Country or the Cause he would vindicate. Not a Poet, by profession or ambition, he has written only at long intervals, or at the instigation of trivial or transient causes. The diversified, and somewhat epigrammatic, character of his writings will evince this. The present volume is composed of occasional effusions, through many years of life. Though thus necessarily individual in their origin and specialties, they become, however, from their multiplicity, general in their adaptations, and give voice to the experiences of many an enthusiastic and imaginative nature. They are marked by varying degrees of ability, and frequent alternations of taste and sentiment. Still it is hoped that they will strike sympathetic chords in appreciative bosoms, and tend to show the richness of the section of the Union, to which they refer, in poetic elements and attributes, which more gifted capacities may hereafter develope, and wreathe into the garlands of a graceful and becoming literature.

The author submits this volume to the public, with a painful sense of its faults and deficiencies, and with the sole wish that its sins and short-comings may be visited upon his head, and not upon the fair portion of our country, whose adaptability for poetic illustration, he has so imperfectly attempted to portray.

It may be well to add that the pieces in this collection are but a meagre selection from the writings of the author, and that most of them have heretofore been published, and have received the verdict of periodical criticism. Some of them have been widely circulated over fictitious names, and one of them (the ode entitled "Balaklava") was attributed, by some error of the press, to a distinguished foreign author—Alexander Smith. It is but due to all parties that the fugitives should be reclaimed, and "held to service" by their proper owner.

INDEX.

SONGS OF THE SOUTH:

SONGS OF THE SOUTH, *Continued:*

POEMS OF THE SOUTH:

POEMS OF THE SOUTH, *Continued:*

POEMS OF THE SOUTH, *Continued:*

SONGS OF THE SOUTH.

ERRATA.

Page 66, line 9. - - - - For *are* read *art*.
" 67, " 14. - - - - - For *Than* read *Then*.
" 74, " 7. - - - - For *it* read *that*.
" 86, " 5. - - - - - For *come* read *came*.
" 128, " 3. - - - - For *heart* read *art*.
" 181. " 7. - - - - - For *When* read *Where*.
" 185, " 17. - - - - Add *now*, at the end.
" 191. " 7. - - - - - Transpose *only* before *in*.
" 205. " 6. - - - - For *smiled* read *united*.
" 218. " 7. - - - - - Transpose *With* and *What* in next line.
" 232, last line. - - - - For *this* read *the*.
" 241, line 3 from bottom. For *need* read *new*.
" 254, " 3. - - - - - For *lover* read *loved*.
" 254, " 13. - - - - - For *art* read *are*.

TO

GEN. MIRABEAU B. LAMAR,

EX-PRESIDENT OF TEXAS,

THE SOLDIER, STATESMAN AND POET:

These Songs,

WHICH HE HAS SO KINDLY APPROVED,

ARE AFFECTIONATELY DEDICATED.

SONGS OF THE SOUTH.

COME TO THE SOUTH.

Oh, come to the South, sweet, beautiful one,
'Tis the clime of the heart, 'tis the shrine of the sun;
Where the sky ever shines with a passionate glow,
And flowers spread their treasures of crimson and snow;
Where the breeze, o'er bright waters, wafts incense along,
And gay birds are glancing in beauty and song;
Where summer smiles ever o'er mountain and plain,
And the best gifts of Eden, unshadowed, remain.

Oh, come to the South,
The shrine of the sun;
And dwell in its bowers,
Sweet, beautiful one.

Oh, come to the South, and I'll build thee a home,
Where winter shall never intrusively come,
The queen-like catalpa, the myrtle and pine,
The gold-fruited orange, the ruby-gemmed vine,
Shall bloom 'round thy dwelling, and shade thee at noon,
While birds of all music keep amorous tune ;
By the gush of glad fountains we'll rest us at eve,
No trouble to vex us, no sorrows to grieve.

Oh, come to the South, &c.

Oh, come to the South, 'tis the home of the heart—
No sky like its own can deep passion impart ;
The glow of its summer is felt in the soul,
And love keepeth ever his fervent control.
Oh, here would thy beauty most brilliantly beam,
And life pass away like some delicate dream ;
Each wish of thy heart should realized be,
And this beautiful land seem an Eden to thee.

Then, come to the South,
The shrine of the sun ;
And dwell in its bowers,
Sweet, beautiful one.

THE MOCKING BIRD.

From the vale, what music ringing,
  Fills the bosom of the night;
On the sense, entrancéd, flinging
  Spells of witchery and delight!
O'er magnolia, lime and cedar,
  From yon locust-top, it swells,
Like the chant of serenader,
  Or the rhymes of silver bells!
      Listen! dearest, listen to it!
        Sweeter sounds were never heard!
      'Tis the song of that wild poet—
        Mime and minstrel—Mocking-Bird.

See him, swinging in his glory,
  On yon topmost bending limb!
Carolling his amorous story,
  Like some wild crusader's hymn!
Now it faints in tones delicious
  As the first low vow of love!

Now it bursts in swells capricious,
All the moonlit vale above!
Listen! dearest, &c.

Why is't thus, this sylvan Petrarch
Pours all night his serenade?
'Tis for some proud woodland Laura,
His sad sonnets all are made!
But he changes now his measure—
Gladness bubbling from his mouth—
Jest, and gibe, and mimic pleasure—
Winged Anacreon of the South!
Listen! dearest, &c.

Bird of music, wit and gladness,
Troubadour of sunny climes,
Disenchanter of all sadness,---
Would thine art were in my rhymes.
O'er the heart that's beating by me,
I would weave a spell divine;
Is there aught she could deny me,
Drinking in such strains as thine?
Listen! dearest, &c.

THE MEXICAN SEA.

Oh! come to the sycamore, maiden, with me!
The stars are awake on the Mexican Sea,—
The breath of the orange, the myrtle and lime,
Gives sweets to the sky of this delicate clime,—
The song of the mocking-bird rings from the trees,
And coolness and beauty are out on the breeze:
Then come to the sycamore, maiden, with me,
And watch the stars float on the Mexican Sea!

Oh! come to the sycamore, maid, and I'll tell
A story was breathed by a coral-lipped shell;
It told of a knight of this passionate land,
Who long sought the boon of a fair lady's hand.
The lady was cruel; his visions all o'er,
He wandered, one night, to this broad sycamore;
In its shadow he stood as I now with thee,
And watched the stars weep o'er the Mexican Sea!

The lady was fair as the sky of her clime;
Her voice had the tune of its sweet waters' chime;
The light of her brow, the magnolia had given;
The violet smiled in her eyes' happy heaven;

Her blushes were caught from the roses of dawn ;
The grace of her motion, the glide of the swan ;
But none of these charms for that lover could be,
And he slept in despair 'neath the Mexican Sea !

Then under the sycamore, here by the sea,
That thou art that lady, I'd whisper to thee,
And I the bold knight, who--but start, not my love--
The stars are now holding *their* nuptials above !
Why not 'mid the sweets of this silver-rimmed night,
Make the heart of thy lover as happy and bright ?
Ah, yes !—'tis enough !—our Eden shall be
The sycamore shade by the Mexican Sea !

GIRL OF THE SUNNY SOUTH.

Girl of the sunny South,
Bright, round thy rosy mouth,
Dimples and smiles are ever at play:
Sweet in thy fountain eyes,
Mirrored, the azure skies
Tell us of angels and heaven alway!

Sunbeams, in golden twine,
Over some pearly shrine,
Emblem thy curls placed carefully by:
Never the lily meek
Blushed with so pure a cheek,
Tinged by the rays of an evening sky.

Sweet is thy laughing tone
As the low music blown
Out of an ocean shell by the sea-maids;
Soft, over heart and soul,
Steals it with deep control,
Leading them rapt through Love's sunny glades!

Ne'er did, on mountain lake,
Swan the wild mirror break,
Gliding in motion so graceful as thine,—
Lark on the summer sky,
Breeze 'mid the bending rye,
Fountain through flowers, are not so divine!

Bright as thy native clime,
Decked in its vernal time,
Girl of the South, in all things you seem!
Ever thus sweetly shine,
Cinctured by light divine,—
Poetry's sunniest, fondest dream!

THE FIELDS OF MEXICO.

The American Maiden's Song to her Lover.

Would'st thou have me love thee, dearest,
With a woman's proudest heart,
Which shall ever hold thee nearest,
Shrined within its inmost part ?—
Listen then !—thy country's calling
On her sons to meet her foe !
Leave these groves of rose and myrtle !—
Drop the dreamy harp of love !—
Like young Körner, scorn the turtle,
While the eagle screams above !—
Haste ! where Freedom's sons are falling
On the fields of Mexico !

Dost thou pause ?—Let dotards dally—
Do *thou* for thy country fight !
'Neath her starry emblem, rally—
"God ! our Country ! and her Right !"
Listen now !—her trumpet's calling
On her sons to meet her foe !
Woman's heart is soft and tender,
But 'tis proud and faithful too !

Shall *she* be her land's defender!
Lover!—Soldier!—up and do!—
Haste away!—where *men* are falling
On the fields of Mexico!

Seize thy father's ancient falchion,
Which once flashed as freedom's star!
Till sweet Peace,—the bow and halcyon,—
Stilled the stormy strife of war!
Listen now!—thy country's calling
On her sons to meet her foe!
Sweet is love in moonlit bowers!—
Sweet the altar and the flame!—
Sweet is spring-time with her flowers!—
Sweeter far the patriot's name!
Haste! then haste! brave hearts are falling
On the fields of Mexico!

Wreaths of fame and smiles of beauty
Will repay the warrior's deeds!
Shall a quibble sully duty,
When an outraged country pleads?
Hark! then hark!—her trump is calling
On her sons to meet her foe!

Now our loved and trophied banner
Floats where Cortez' eagles flew !—
Shall the hordes of Santa Anna
Stain its field of starry blue ?—
Haste ! thy brethren now are falling
On the fields of Mexico !

Should the God who rules above thee,
Doom thee to a soldier's grave,
Hearts will break !—but Fame will love thee,
Canonized among the brave !—
Listen then !—thy country's calling
On her sons to meet her foe !—
Rather would I view thee lying
On the last red field of life,
'Mid thy country's heroes dying,
Than to be a dastard's wife !—
Haste then, love ! where men are falling
On the fields of Mexico !

But my heart grows now a prophet,
And beholds afar thy brow,
With young glory's star above it,
Safe returned, before me bow !

Listen then !—thy country 's calling
On her sons to meet her foe !—
Leave these groves of rose and myrtle !—
Drop the the dreamy harp of love !—
Like young Körner, scorn the turtle,
When the eagle screams above !—
Haste ! where Freedom's sons are falling
On the fields of Mexico !

THE LAND THAT WE LIVE IN!

Oh! bright is the land that we live in,
  And soft blow the breezes around—
The stars make a palace of heaven,
  And flowers enamel the ground!
The orange and chestnut are flinging
  Their odors divine on the gale,
And the mocking-bird's melody's ringing
  From bowers that circle the vale!
    Then here's to the land that we live in!—
      The land of the locust and lime!—
    And a song for the sweet stars of heaven,
      That brighten this beautiful clime!

But dearer by far to the minstrel,
  Than all the sweet wealth of this land,
Are the maidens who dwell in its bowers,
  By mountain, savanna, and strand!
And all its rich trophies were given,
  As tributes of beauty to these;
And these are the stars of our heaven,—

The flowers that gladden the breeze.
Then here's to the land that we live in !—
The land of the locust and lime !—
And a song for the sweet stars of heaven,
That brighten this beautiful clime !

'Twas hymned by a bard, that the planets
Once, charmed from their passionate home,
Assumed the fair features of women,
And dwelt in the vallies of Rome !
But sure, if a land e'er presented
Temptation to angels, 'tis ours,
And the vision of song was invented
From forms in these soft, sunny bowers !
Then here's to the land that we live in !
The land of the locust and lime !
And a song for the sweet stars of heaven,
That brighten this beautiful clime !

THE SEA—IN CALM AND STORM.

In sunny cove and crescent dell,
The bright green waters sink and swell ;
The dimpled waves lapse on the strand,
And, rippling, kiss the diamond sand ;
Far out, the wild gull on the wave,
Her snowy bosom stoops to lave ;
Soft glides the breeze, and all the sea
Lies lulled in sweet tranquility !

But now away, the waves are stirred,
And, shrieking, darts the wild sea-bird ;
The snow-caps on the billows' verge,
Are tossed in fury by the surge ;
The storm is up, and o'er the deep
His angry pinions rushing sweep ;
The breakers crash along the shore,
And echo back the thunder's roar !

An hour agone, upon the sea,
A gallant ship swung merrily ;
The morning breeze, in odors sweet,
Just dallied with her canvass sheet ;

Light hearts leaned o'er her pictured side,
To watch the cleft waves 'round her glide;
And song and laugh rose on the breeze,
To bless the Sabbath of the seas!

But now the storm! the mighty storm!
Bursts 'round that vessel's fragile form!
Her shivering spars are snapped in twain;
Her hulk drives madly o'er the main;
God help her crew! their gurgling cry
Peals faintly through the thundering sky;
She's dashed upon the craggy shore,
And sinks amid the breakers' roar!

'Tis thus the sea! the bright blue sea!
The home of high hearts, bold and free!
Smiles in her beauty, like a bride,
To greet the tall ship's graceful glide;
But lashed to fury by the storm,
What mountain waves her breast deform!
Man's proudest strength quails at her nod,
The image of an angry God!

MAGNOLIA GROVE.

When busy day's rude cares are done,
And on the sea descends the sun ;
When hues of crimson, green and gold,
Thro' twilight's heaven like waves are rolled,
And sky and sea and bird and flower
Feel the soft influence of the hour :
How sweet amid thy bowers to rove,
With one we love, Magnolia Grove !

The tall trees robed in spring-time's green,
Like monarchs, stand amid the scene !
While broad white flowers their brows begem,
Each like a jeweled diadem !
Below the honey-suckle shines,
'Mid rich festoons of glittering vines,
And paroquets,—gay babblers,—move
Through all thine aisles, Magnolia Grove !

The blue Bay sweetly spreads before,
And laves, like love, that beauteous shore ;
Each rippling wave, with gentlest speech,
Makes music on the sandy beach ;

While in the deep, 'mid clearer skies,
The halcyon scene, reflected, lies :
Could fancy's Edens brighter prove
Than thy fair bowers, Magnolia Grove ?

Bright memories, too, to thee belong,
And through thy bowers, at twilight throng.
Here roved the dark-eyed Choctaw maid,
And wove her lover's wampum braid ;
Here came the laughing girls of France,
And sunny Spain, with love-lit glance ;
Till, last of all, with hearts more true,
Came eyes that gleam in Saxon blue :
What rapturous scenes of joy and love,
Hast thou beheld, Magnolia Grove !

I, too, have loved at eve to stray
Along the margin of that Bay,
With one beloved,—or to recline
On some enameled, flowery shrine ;
With tales of love to please her ear,
Or list the red bird warbling near :
'Tis past !—but yet where'er I rove,
I'll dream of thee, Magnolia Grove !

THE HEART AND BIRD.

There is a white bird of the sea,
    Beneath our Southern sky,
That ever soaring seems to be,
    Where tossing breezes fly ;
No eye has ever seen him rest ;
No fowler knows his secret nest ;
Yet far away in starry isles,
    That gem the dimpled wave,
Where blue-eyed summer ever smiles,
    And pearls the waters pave ;
O'er snowy shells, bright flowers above,
He keeps his hidden nest of love !

My heart is like that Southern bird ;
    Its pinions cannot rest
Amid these scenes where naught is heard
    But idle song and jest ;
It sports around with fluttering wing ;
It seems a gay unthoughted thing :

But far away it has a shrine,
  Hid from the vulgar gaze,
Where nature's brighest beauties shine
  Around an angel face :
There, like that restless ocean-dove,
It keeps its hidden nest of love !

Yes, dearest, though afar from me,
  Thou art my only joy,
A green isle in life's sunniest sea,
  Far from this wild annoy.
Oh, would my weary heart could fly,
To greet thy blue beloved eye !
Then bowered in bliss, from care remote,
  Our lives, in peace and pride,
Like yon sun-tinted barque, should float
  Adown the future's tide !
Bird of the ocean soar above !
Mine is a sweeter nest of love !

NOT AGAIN.

Not again, not again
Can my heart its dream renew !
Brighter forms may meet my view ;
Sweeter voices wander by,
With a dreamier melody ;
Spirits beckon through the trees,
White robes flashing on the breeze ;
But they lure and tempt in vain ;
My sad heart will wear its chain
Not again !

Not again, not again !
Wine that on the sand is poured
To the cup may be restored :
Fragrance, on the wild breeze shed,
Bless the floweret whence it sped ;
Music seek the broken lute,
Long forgotten, longer mute :
But the heart once quell'd by pain,
Can its early bliss attain
Not again !

Not again, not again !
Tempt me then no more, sweet girl,
To imbibe the liquid pearl !
Though your face might win a saint
From his temple's dim restraint,
Yet my heart, while owning this,
Turns insensate from the bliss ;
In its gloom it must remain,
Doomed to smile in beauty's train
Not again !

Not again, not again !
For, in bright and trusting youth,
Wounded was my bosom's truth :
O'er my heart was thrown a spell
Stronger than weak words can tell ;
And a face, as angel's bright,
Darkened Hope's devoted light :
Joy to me since then is vain,
I can trust Love's syren strain
Not again !

THE ROSE OF ALABAMA.

I loved, in boyhood's happy time,
When life was like a minstrel's rhyme,
And cloudless as my native clime,
The Rose of Alabama.
Oh, lovely rose!
The sweetest flower earth knows,
Is the Rose of Alabama!

One pleasant, balmy night in June,
When swung, in silvery clouds, the moon,
My heart awoke love's vesper tune,
For Rose of Alabama!

She caught the strain, and to the bower,
Impelled by love and music's power,
Stole like an angel, at that hour,
The Rose of Alabama!

Beside me there her form she placed,
My arm stole gently 'round her waist,
And earth seemed with new beauty graced,
By Rose of Alabama!

The breeze and streamlet ceased their tone ;
Like winged gems the fire-flies shone ;
The flowers gazed envious on my own
Sweet Rose of Alabama !

'Tis vain our mutual vows to tell—
One strain upon my plaintive shell,
And then I bade a sad farewell
To Rose of Alabama !

Long years have passed ; by fortune driven,
I wander 'neath a stranger heaven ;
But, ah ! love's ties are not yet riven
From Rose of Alabama !

Hope smiles upon my pilgrim way,
Ere long my feet shall homeward stray,
And time bring round my nuptial day
With Rose of Alabama !

Then, shrine-like, in my native land,
Love's Eden ! shall my cottage stand,
With happiness on every hand !
Sweet Rose of Alabama !

BEAUTY, SONG AND LOVE.

Long, in sorrow's gloomy night,
Had my heart deserted lain,
When thy face, like sweet moonlight,
Brightened all its sky again !
There was round thee such a glow,
Like the air where angels move,
That my heart dawned from its woe,
And all was beauty, all was love !

Once I knew a silver tone,
Sweeter than an angel's hymn,—
It from earth methought had flown,
Flown to join the seraphim !
But thy voice recalled the spell,
Melody unmatched above,—
On my heart its influence fell,
And all was music, all was love !

Shall that gloom again return ?
Shall this music cease from me ?

Is my heart aye doomed to learn,
  Beauty's smile is misery?
Lady fair, the answer—thine,
  Thine the destiny to prove;
Frown, my heart will cease to shine—
  But smile,—'tis music, light and love!

THE GOLDEN BOWL IS BROKEN.

The golden bowl is broken,
 That held love's rosy wine ;
The last fond words are spoken,
 That hailed thee once as mine:
We're fated now to sever,
 Yet on the land or sea,
By day or night, forever,
 My heart will kneel to thee !
  Though the golden bowl be broken,
   My heart will kneel to thee !

The silver chord is silent,
 That thrilled beneath thy hand ;
As in some desert island,
 'Mid fallen hopes I stand !
But yet where'er I wander,
 Thy beauty I shall see,
And as the past, I ponder,
 My heart will kneel to thee !
  Though the silver chord be silent,
   My heart will kneel to thee !

Oh ! each imperfect token
  Is vain my love to tell ;
Though the golden bowl be broken,
  And the silver chord as well ;
Fond memory will cherish
  The dreams so dear to me,
And till each pulse shall perish,
  My heart will kneel to thee !
    Though the golden bowl be broken,
      My heart will kneel to thee.

THE BELLE OF MOBILE.

The roses in Spring, their rich fragrance may fling,
  And beauty and song on the senses may steal,
But there's naught in the air, or the earth can compare,
  Young and lovely and fair, with the Belle of Mobile!

Her lips and her eyes are like gems from the skies;
  Some seraph has set on her forehead his seal;
And a radiant grace, time can never displace,
  Is enthroned on the face of the Belle of Mobile!

Through dreams of delight, in some soft summer night,
  Bright angels descending, their beauty reveal;
But more glowing and warm, and more rich in each charm,
  Is the ripe rounded form of the Belle of Mobile!

The raptures of song to her voice belong,
  Whose tones to your heart will enchantingly steal:
While the spells of her mind, by each virtue refined,
  Will the witchery bind of the Belle of Mobile!

The East and the West are of fair forms possessed ;
  The hills of the Northland proud maidens conceal;
But in beauty and soul, far excelling the whole,
  Is the lovely Creole, the bright Belle of Mobile !

"LOOK NOT ON THE WINE WHEN IT IS RED."

A TEMPERANCE SONG.

Oh! look not on the wine when red—
  When sparkling in the crystal cup—
For though bright hues are 'round it spread,
  'Twill burn thy priceless spirit up!
The dark-browed queen of Egypt gave
Her richest jewels to its wave;
And, as they perished, in the bowl
Will sink the treasures of thy soul!

Oh, look not on the crimson wine!
  Let not its waters kiss thy lips;
For, in their gay, delusive shine,
  There's hidden death for him who sips!
The olden fount, the prophet viewed,
Gleamed brightly in the solitude;
But soon, for him who drank, a grave
Was found by Marah's bitter wave!

Oh, look not on the treacherous wine,
  When mantling in the jeweled bowl;

Though wreaths and flowers around it twine,
They breathe a poison on the soul!
The orient Upas proudly waves
Its foliage o'er a land of graves!
And thus the flower-wreathed goblet's breath
Brings desolation, woe, and death!

Oh, look not on the tempting wine!
Pass not beneath its syren rod,
Nor bow before its dæmon shrine,
The image of creation's God!
It is the fabled Circé bowl
That dwarfed the stature, drowned the soul,
And, by its sorcery, fell though mute,
Transformed the angel to the brute!

Oh, look not on the wine when red!
It is the deadliest human foe;
It wreathes a cypress 'round the head,
And lays the proudest trophies low!
It darkens virtue, poisons health,
Blasts peace and hope, and robs of wealth;
Crime, Pain, and Famine 'round it tread—
Then look not on the wine when red!

A VALENTINE.

The morning beams are sprinkling
  With gems, the dewy green ;
The early bells are tinkling,
  Where grazing herds are seen ;
Bright birds are swiftly winging
  Their circling flights above,
And every grove is ringing
  With melodies of love !
    Then, sweet one, kindly listen !
      Oh, list this song of mine !
    And, as thy blue eyes glisten,
      Make me thy *Valentine !*

How sweet this golden morning !
  This Love-Day of the year !
When, nature's face adorning,
  The brightest smiles appear !
When love is made a duty,
  From immemorial time,
And, ever, generous beauty
  Has loved the minstrel's rhyme !

Then, sweet one, kindly listen !
Oh, list this song of mine !
And, as thy blue eyes glisten,
Own me, thy *Valentine!*

Thy beauty is the brightest
Of all beheld to-day :
Thy footstep is the lightest
That o'er the flowers may stray ;
Love never found a dwelling
More gentle than thy heart ;
All other forms excelling,
Love's Paragon thou art !
Then, sweet one, kindly listen !
Oh, list this song of mine !
And, as thy blue eyes glisten,
Smile on thy *Valentine!*

This land of myrtle blossoms,
This clime of sun and soul,
Where love, o'er swelling bosoms,
Exerts supreme control,
Would be all cold and lonely,
In vain its flowers and rays,

If from my worship, only
  Was hid thine angel face !
    Then, sweet one, kindly listen !
      Oh, list this song of mine !
    And, as thy blue eyes glisten,
      Oh, bless thy *Valentine!*

SONG AT THE BAR DINNER.

Ye sons of Blackstone, Chitty, Coke,
  Of Marshall, Kent, and Story,
Come join awhile in song and joke,
  In mirth and festive glory :
Put by your summons, writs and pleas,
  Your briefs and declarations,
And for a season, take your ease
  In feastings and libations !

What though your lady-love, the Law,
  Is grave, sedate and solemn,
And seldom can refreshment draw
  But from some musty volume :—
Yet she, herself, will now decline
  Each dull and knotty question,—
Desert her *Viner*, for the *Vine*,
  The *Digest*, for *digestion !*

The drone, who, over *Doe* and *Roe*,
  Can only feed his fancies,
Will find at last his cake all *dough*,—
  His readings all *ro*-mances :

But he, who bends o'er "cakes and ale,"
  As well as Clay, and Aikin,
Will prove himself both *Swift* and *Hale*,
  And doubly "save his *Bacon!*"

Then put the *green bag* in its place,—
  Light with your *tape* these *tapers*,—
Exchange your *cases* for this *case*
  Of wines, cigars, and capers:
"A deed," indeed, "is doing now,"
  Worth all your *deeds* indented,—
Reporters here to *porters* bow,—
  Don't be *non est invent*-ed!

Come file your *pleas* before this Court,
  Where all my *please on trial*,—
You can't *demur*, not e'en *in short*,
  So come,—there's no denial:
This is the *Bar*,—straight *traverse* join,—
  Your *fee* is in your pocket,—
Crave oyer quickly, of—this wine,—
  Or—*strike him from the docket!*

These dishes are in *season* all,
  So make at once your *seizin*—

To disobey "*Law's* serious call,"
Is mutiny—nay, treason :
You can't *desert* without *dessert*—
'Twould shame your high profession—
So while of mirth, we make *profert,*
Reduce it to possession!

The sons of Themis in Mobile—
A numerous generation—
Once more have met, for common weal,
To keep this celebration :
Grave judges now desert the Bench,
Old lawyers leave their cases,
And students turn from Norman-French,
To meet with merry faces !

Then throw the dull reports aside—
Let Johnson sleep with Peters—
Let *Porter* prove a liquid tide,
And *Stuart* feast the eaters !
One day we'll give to song and wit,
Ad mala usque ovo,
And then resume the *brief* and *writ,*
And try the Law, *de novo.*

OH! COME BACK SOON.

Oh, come back soon, oh, come back soon!
  My heart is sad without thee,
There is no light in sun or moon,
  So sweet as that about thee.
The sky looks cold, the breezes sigh,
  Each scene is dark and lonely;
Earth holds for me no peace or joy,
  But in thy presence only!

Oh, come back soon, oh, come back soon!
  Though other hearts may greet thee,
With smile and song and pleasure's tune,
  None half so fond will meet thee.
Tho' kind and fervent they may prove,
  When festal cups are flowing,
They ne'er can feel the constant love
  That in my breast is glowing!

Oh, come back soon, oh, come back soon,
  Back to these sylvan bowers;

When thou art far, there is no boon
  Can cheer the lonely hours.
Return and they will glide away,
  Like dreams of sweetest pleasure,
And thou shalt prove the strength of love
  No earthly bounds can measure.

DIRGE.

Sung at the Obsequies to Henry Clay, at Mobile.

With drooping flag, with muffled drum,
Amid a nation's gloom we come,—
For, from the earth, has passed away
The patriot soul of HENRY CLAY.

As children 'round a parent meet,
And, sobbing, grasp his winding sheet,
So millions now, o'erwhelmed with grief,
Bewail their loved, their fallen chief.

Long 'mid our gallant, great and good,
Like WASHINGTON, he nobly stood,
While, trembling on his burning tongue,
Truth, justice, peace and freedom hung.

Thrice, when our storm-tossed Ship of State
Seemed sinking with its priceless freight,
His guardian spirit, firm and free,
Walked o'er our troubled Galilee!

Through all the world, his glorious name
Is whispered by the lips of fame ;
For long, in every kindling zone,
His voice was Freedom's bugle-tone.

The Greek girl, kneeling by her seas,
Deemed him a new Demosthenes,
And young Bolivar's patriot ray
Was, light-like, caught from HENRY CLAY.

Oh Father, Chieftain, Statesman, Sage,
The pride, the glory of our age,—
Athwart our land a gloom is spread,
Our country's Second Sire is dead !

Well may yon bannered stars grow dim,
Yon stooping eagle mourn for him,
For when such sunlike spirits die,
Darkness should veil the land and SKY.

Yet still his fame shall shine through years,
The Iris of our country's tears,—
And from our hearts ne'er fade away
The deathless name of HENRY CLAY.

ODE IN MEMORY OF WEBSTER.

Sung at his Obsequies in Mobile.

From the sky of our country, a sun has descended !
  A pillar has fallen in Liberty's fane :
The Pharos, whose beams o'er the ocean extended,
  No longer is seen by the desolate main !
Thick darkness and sorrow encompass the nation,
  The Genius of Freedom disconsolate sighs,
And bends, with her children, in deep tribulation,
  Around the low couch where her champion lies !

Great WEBSTER has fallen—the grand and the peerless,
  The statesman with love to no section confined,
The orator matchless, the patriot fearless,
  The giant of learning, the Titan of mind.
The Pride of the Nation in silence reposes,
  And o'er his pale form her last tribute she gives,
But still, as with sadness, his coffin she closes,
  She feels his own words, *He still lives ! He still lives !*

He lives on the pages of freedom forever,
  He lives in the deathless dominion of mind,
He lives in his lofty conceptions that never
  Can fade from the homage or love of mankind !
The grave unto him was the portal to glory,
  His fame is a pyramid piled to the sky,
And never, while greatness is cherished in story,
  The genius and virtues of WEBSTER can die !

THE SWAN.

O'er the lake, how sweetly gliding,
  Yonder proud and snowy swan,
Every restless billow chiding,
  Moves in graceful beauty on !
So, above the tides of feeling,—
  Tides that in my bosom move, –
Passion's rude commotion stilling,—
  Moves thy spirit, Lady-Love !

'Round that swan, what light and beauty
  Shine along the am'rous tide,
Brightening all things with their presence—
  Sky, and wave, and forest-side !
So, within my lonely bosom,—
  Soft as moonlight from above,—
Beams a mild, celestial halo
  'Round thy spirit, Lady-Love !

Now, with rich, exultant music,
  List ! yon fair bird charms the scene !

Joy receiving,—joy conferring,—
  Song and beauty's magic queen!
Thus, to crown thine own enchantment,
  Like some seraph from above,
Fill my heart with hope's glad anthems,
  Beauteous spirit, Lady-Love!

DO I LOVE THEE?

Do I love thee?—Ask the flowers
  If they love the breath of Spring,—
Ask them if the morning hours
  Fragrant dew and freshness bring,—
List their answer!—Such to me
Is the love I feel for thee!

Do I love thee?—Does the rover,
  Wrecked upon the stormy strand,
Love, when help and hope were over,
  Safely on the shore to stand?
So I love to cling to thee,
Love's fair isle in sorrow's sea!

Do I love thee?—Are the places
  Angel-trod, to pilgrims dear?
Is the cool and green oasis
  Welcome in the desert drear?
Fonder is my love for thee,—
Dearer is thy love to me.

Do I love thee?—If devotion
  Be of love the surest test,—
If the rivers love the ocean,
  Drawn by instinct to its breast,—
Then my heart in homage see,—
All its currents flow to thee!

CHOCTAW MELODIES.

I.

A MOTHER'S DIRGE FOR HER INFANT.

In a small grove of dogwood trees,
Whose spring-time flowers perfumed the breeze,
By Pascagoula's tawny wave,
There was a little new-made grave.
And there above the humble mound
A youthful mother oft was found,
Who thus, in sad and frantic strains,
Wept o'er her first-born babe's remains :

"Now cradled in the damp cold ground,
My little warior lies ;
Now he is bound with wampum round,
And shut his sparkling eyes :
Yet why, above his place of sleep,—
Why should I weep?

"The little bird, when it is grown,
Must leave its native nest,
'Mid snares and foes to soar alone,
By want and care distrest;
And oft the cruel hunter's dart
Will pierce its heart.

"But thou, sweet one, hast shed no tears,
Nor felt the woes of life;
Thy spirit, undisturbed by fears,
By anguish and by strife,
To golden groves has soared above,
Bird of my love!

"Ah! hadst thou only staid below,
What grace and strength were thine,
To chase the dear, to bend the bow,
To draw the fisher's line!
Or bravely in the battle-field
The club to wield!

"Yet why should I lament thy doom?
The bud, that in the Spring-time dies,
Bears all its bloom and sweet perfume
To spirits in the skies!

A heavenly blossom now thou art,
Bud of my heart!

"But oh thou wert to young to go,—
Thy little tender feet
No father's guidance now can know,
No mother's counsel meet.
Who now will nurse thy fragile form,
And keep thee warm?

"Ah! yes, I hear a spirit say
I will protect him here—
Who from their cradles pass away,
To us are ever dear.
Then why my babe above thy sleep—
Why should I weep?"

II.

ATALA'S LAMENT.

[From the French of Chateaubriand.]

The Indian maiden turned at eve,
In exiled loneliness to grieve,

And shed, by Mississippi's side,
Her tears upon its turbid tide;
For she had left in passion's hours,
Her Florida's beloved bowers,
And thus, amid the stranger throng,
Poured forth an exile's plaintive song:

"Oh, happy they who ne'er have seen
The smoke of alien fires!
Nor guests at other feasts have been,
Than their own sires'!
Ah! should the blue-jay of the West
Say to the Southern nonpareil,
'Why not amid our branches rest?
Why only mourning numbers tell?
Have we not limpid waters here—
Delightful shades, abundant food,
And flowery fields, and orchards fair,
As you have in your native wood?'
Yet would the stray bird answer then,
'My nest is in the jasmine grove!
Oh, give my golden skies agen,
And bright savannahs that I love!'

" Oh, happy they who ne'er have seen
The smoke of alien fires,
Nor guests at other feasts have been,
Than their own sires'!
When, after hours of toil and pain,
The weary traveler sinks at night,
And sees anear him, on the plain,
Fair cottages with many a light;
In vain he views their pleasant glow—
No hospitable fare they yield—
For, should he enter with his bow,
All welcome is at once concealed;
Again his sturdy bow he takes,
And, weak, insulted, turns away,
And totters on through tangled brakes,
And deserts wide till dawn of day.

" Oh, happy they who ne'er have seen
The smoke of alien fires,
Nor guests at other feasts have been,
Than their own sires'!
Dear stories round the social hearth!
Soft songs with tenderest feelings rife!

Pure deeds of love, and tones of mirth,
  So needful in this weary life !—
Ye, ye have filled the days of those
  Who ne'er their parent land have left,—
Who ne'er have been, 'mid stranger foes,
  Of all that's best on earth bereft !
They live in bliss, and when life ends,
  Their graves are in their mother's breast ;
By setting suns and tears of friends,
  And fair religion sweetly blest !
    Oh, happy they who ne'er have seen
      The smoke of alien fires,
    Nor guests at other feasts have been,
      Than their own sires'!"

OH, DO NOT CEASE TO LOVE ME.

Oh, do not cease to love me !
  My heart so clings to thee,
That not the heavens above me,
  Nor wealth of earth and sea,
Nor all the starry flowers,
In Spring-time's golden hours,
  That bloom along the lea,
  Are half so dear to me !

Oh, do not cease to love me !
  For many weary years,
Thy smile has shone above me,
  The rainbow of my tears !
Thy love has been my treasure,—
My bosom's only pleasure,—
  Its light 'mid griefs and fears,
  For many weary years !

Oh, do not cease to love me !
  Let wealth and fame depart,—

All other joys that move me,
  Desert my lonely heart,—
But, day-spring of my gladness,
My charm in every sadness,
  Let not thy love depart,
  Bright mistress of my heart!

THE HOMES OF ALABAMA.

I.

The homes of Alabama,
  How beautiful they rise,
Throughout her queenly forest realm,
  Beneath her smiling skies!
The richest odors fill the breeze,
  Her vallies teem with wealth,
And the homes of Alabama,
  Are the rosy homes of health!

II.

The homes of Alabama,—
  The cottage and the hall,—
Her institutions spread alike
  A guardian care o'er all!—
No titled fopling spurns aside
  The peasant from his way,
But the homes of Alabama
  Are blessed by equal sway!

III.

The homes of Alabama,
  The prairie's flowery bed,—
The broad fields decked with snowy wreaths,—
  The mountain's star-crowned head:
The forest and the fertile soil,
  Each, all, their tributes bring,
And the homes of Alabama,
  Teem with the offering!

IV.

The homes of Alabama,
  The shrines of Faith and Love,
Where honest hearts forever lift
  Their incense-prayers above!
Where science, art and peace combine
  To scatter bliss around,
And make the once rude savage wastes
  Now consecrated ground!

V.

The homes of Alabama,
  Homes of the Brave and Free,—

Stout hearts beneath their cabin roofs
  Pulsate with liberty !
They scorn the despot's iron rule,
  The zealot's galling chain,—
And the homes of Alabama
  Shall ever free remain !

VI.

The homes of Alabama,
  Let the tyrant keep his own,
The bigot nurse his narrow creed,
  But not pollute her zone !
Should War and Frenzy ever strive
  To crush her strength, they'll feel
That the homes of Alabama
  Are filled by hearts of steel !

THE MOTHERS OF THE SOUTH.

The Mothers of the South !
 In the lurid morn of Battle,
When, from the cannon's mouth,
 Came the thunder's deadly rattle,—
Their fair and fragile forms
 Shrank not, in terror, from us,
But,—rainbows on the storms !—
 Still gave us freedom's promise !
Then pledge, to-night, their memories bright,
 Our noble Southern mothers !
Who in the strife,—maid, matron, wife,—
 Stood by their sons and brothers !

On Camden's fatal plain,
 At Eutaw and Savannah,
The star of freedom's train
 Was beauty's woven banner !
Throughout the night of woe,
 That flag was still resplendent,
And many a son fell low,
 To keep its folds ascendant !

Then pledge, to-night, their memories bright,
  Our noble Southern mothers !
Who in the strife,—maid, matron, wife,—
  Stood by their sons and brothers !

Oh, yes ! we'll keep their names
  Embalmed in song and story,—
Those lion-hearted dames,
  Who cradled freedom's glory :
And, should the strife of war
  E'er tinge again our waters,
We'll find, our hearts to cheer,
  Those matrons in their daughters !
Then pledge, to-night, their memories bright,
  Our noble Southern mothers !
Who in the strife,—maid, matron, wife,—
  Stood by their sons and brothers !

ANACREONTIC.

Come, fill up the cup to the girl you love best!
To her eyes, and her lips, and her innocent breast:
To her eyes, that, as soft as these young bubbles shine,
That sparkle and float through the gold of this wine:
To her lips that are dewed with a nectar of bliss,—
Like roses in Spring-time, more fragrant than this:
And her innocent breast, where the young Virtues keep,
'Neath snow-heaving billows, a home in the deep!
Then fill up the cup,
With pleasure and zest,
And pledge, in a bumper,
The girl you love best!

Oh! who for the pleasures of wealth would repine!
If blest with *her* heart,—love's delicate shrine!
A vine-trellised cot, by the side of a stream,
In the light of her smiles, a proud palace would seem!
And, life, like the song that she warbled at even,
'Neath the hush of the sunset, glide gently to heaven!

Ah! pleasure is found by those spirits alone,
Who melt, like twin-streams of the valley, in one!
Then fill up the cup, &c.

The scholar may burn for the laurels of fame,
The altar will sink 'neath the heat of the flame:
The hero may yearn for posterity's smile,—
His heart will be lonely and starless the while:
True bliss, whether here or in heaven above,
Is alone to be found with the angels we love!
One kiss from the lips of fond Woman is worth
All the laurels of fame, or the plaudits of earth!
Then fill up the cup, &c.

Yes! a bumper to beauty! and oh, as you sip,
Let the bright waters linger awhile on your lip:
The queen of the East in her cup dropt a pearl,
But here is the *heart* of your beautiful girl!
Her eyes shed their smiles through these waters of bliss,
And you dream, as you drink, of the first stolen kiss!
Oh, soon may that dream prove a vision of truth,
And beauty recline on the bosom of Youth!
Then fill up the cup, &c.

THE QUEEN OF MAY.

Bring flowers to crown the lovely Queen !
  Bring flowers from vale and hill,—
Bring flowers from grove, and garden green,
  And from each sylvan rill !
For, oh, it is a joyous time,—
  A bright and festal day,—
And fairest flowers, in wreaths, should twine,
  To crown the Queen of May !

How gaily leaps the spirit forth,
  On such a morn as this !
And sky, and wave, and smiling earth
  Are redolent of bliss !
Spring's sweetest honors spread around,
  And balmy breezes play,—
And many a glad and lovely sound
  Attends the Queen of May !

From distant hill,—from nearer grove,
  The feathered minstrels sing

Their roundelays of bliss and love,—
  The symphony of Spring!
Their songs gush out, with sweetest tone,
  Upon this triumph day,
And gladly mingle with our own,
  To hail the Queen of May!

How brightly shine the Day-God's beams!
  How beautiful the sky
How lovely glance the laughing streams,
  In snow and silver, by!
The bowers are waving fresh and green,
  The flowers are fair and gay,—
Though all are lovely, none are seen,
  Fair as the Queen of May!

Then pour the heart's glad music out,
  In honor to our Queen,—
And hail, with many a joyous shout,
  Th' enchantress of the scene:
Let flowers around her path be spread,
  While we our homage pay,
And place this wreath upon her head,
  Our own, sweet Queen of May!

THE ROSE OF LOVE.

[From Anacreon.]

The Rose of Love! oh let us twine
  Its pictured blossoms 'round the bowl!
And deck our brows with wreaths divine,
  To shed aroma on the soul!—
Then while with merry hearts we laugh,
Will breathe its fragrance as we quaff!

Sweet Rose!—thou are Earth's loveliest flower,—
  The pride and darling of the Spring!—
The Gods themselves confess thy power,
  And poet-lips thy praises sing.
With thee young Cupid crowns his curls
When dancing with the graceful girls!

Then crown me Bacchus, with the rose!
  And, making music at thy shrine,
Some beauteous maiden I will choose,
  Whose rounded breast shall swell to mine.
And 'neath the flowers that o'er us glance
In rosy wreaths, with her I'll dance!

A TROUBADOUR SONG.

The harp, I strung in early youth,
Hath lain in dust so long,
That it hath lost, I fear, in sooth,
The cunning art of song:
Yet, gentle one, I wake once more
Its chords, at thy command,
And sing, like ancient Troubadour,
The Ladye of our Land!

Ah, had the days of Chivalry
Not faded long ago,
What feuds would be, fair one, for thee!—
Brave feuds for thee, I trow!
Than many a Knight would seek the field,
Thy colors in his crest,
Thy name inscribed upon his shield,—
The Loveliest and the Best!

And many a Minstrel then would tune
The harp of love for thee,

And seek, by song, to win the boon,
  Beneath the moonlight tree :
And many a Pilgrim too would come,
  With palm-leaf in his hand,
And ask thy smiles to make it bloom,
  Sweet Ladye of our Land !

But ah, those pictured times have gone,—
  The days of old Romance !—
And woman's love no more is won
  By palm-leaf, lyre, or lance :
We have a plainer way with us,—
  More easy if less grand,
We never *kick up such a fuss*
  About a Ladye's hand !

And yet, fair one, there's many a heart
  Beneath its doublet plain,
That holds for thee as warm a part
  As ever Knight did feign ;
And one fond Minstrel lingers yet,
  Who near thee, aye, would stand,
And sing thy gentle loveliness,
  Sweet Ladye of our Land !

BE HUSHED THE HARP !

Be hushed the harp !—its notes are sad,
  And sorrow breathes in every strain,—
It tells of joys, whose light has fled
  And hopes that ne'er can dawn again !—
When last I heard that thrilling tone,
  My heart was like the summer bee ;
But ah, its summer now has gone,
  And grief alone is left to me !

Be hushed the harp !—its murmurs cease,—
  In silence let its strains repose,—
For oh, they blight the spirit's peace,
  And sadden all the bliss it knows ;—
They wake remembrance from her sleep,
  Her fond forgetfulness of pain,
And drive the stricken heart to weep,
  O'er thoughts that long have buried lain !

Then hush the harp !—or fondly tune
  Its numbers to some lighter lay,—

Some song of pleasures yet to bloom,
  And hope shall conquer Memory !—
Some prophet strain of peace and love,
  And future joys, oh, now be given,
And the lorn heart will look above,
  And lose its grief, in dreams of Heaven !

POEMS.

TO

JOHN W. OVERALL, ESQ.,

OF NEW ORLEANS;

AS A TRIBUTE

OF

Personal and Literary Friendship,

THESE POEMS

ARE INSCRIBED

POEMS.

THE ARTS IDEAL.

I.

The Arts are sisters, we are told,—
  A linked and starry throng,
Who shed o'er earth the softening gold
  Of Painting, Sculpture, Song!
When from the seraph-sentried Gate,
  Man turned in wild despair,
The flowers that decked his loved estate,
  The songs that floated there,
The forms that glimmered though the trees,
  With shining arms and curls,
The wild harps swinging in the breeze,
  The streamlets paved with pearls,—

All these,—the treasures of his life,—
  The joys of sinless love,—
Had vanished from his path of strife,
  And flown to realms above :
But still, upon his darkened heart,
  Their memory delayed,
Like stars it through the night impart
  Beams of the glory fled.
Like stars it shone, and bade him strive
  The glory to restore,
And, on the shadowed earth, revive
  Her morning light once more.
Bold heart !—by wizard genius taught,
  He caught the fire divine,
And once again to earth were brought
  The Arts that speak and shine.
Then Song and graceful Sculpture came,
  And Architecture bold,
And Painting, with her wand of flame,
  Her beauteous robes unrolled.
Fair sisters !—'round their paths they flung
  The radiance of the skies,
And earth again was fair and young,
  And man content and wise !

II.

The Arts *are* sisters : Yes, the same
  High spirit fills them all;
At one pure source each lit her flame,
  And heard one common call.
The graceful angel of our lives,—
  The deity within,—
Who in high hearts her sweetness hives,
  And purifies from sin,—
The soul's IDEAL,—it is her
  Sweet influence gives them birth,—
Each is her graceful minister,
  To beautify the earth.
She tuned the wild-wood harp of Burns,
  And Raphael's pencil fired ;
She lingered o'er Canova's urns,
  And Memnon's stone inspired !
Her torch shed glory 'round Lorraine,
  And sightless Milton led,
Till brighter Edens blessed again
  The earth than that had fled.
Along the Nile they bloomed and shone,
  The " Violet-City" blessed,

And brightened e'en Campania's zone,
  With richer loveliness.
On rugged souls the influence fell,
  And fierce and fiery hearts
Grew soft beneath the holy spell,—
  The Baptism of the Arts!

III.

Such are the Arts,—young Dreamer,* such
  The linked and starry throng,
Who've waked thy heart with prophet-touch,—
  Whose spells to thee belong.
Yes, though the youngest one alone,—
  Sweet Glass of nature's face!—
Hath won thy worship for her own,
  Yet all have given their grace.
For on thy tablets, glowing sweet
  With beauty's morning light,
Where grace, and love, and softness meet,
  And all seems breathing, bright,—
Oh! who can gaze nor feel that there

---

* Addressed to William C. Saunders, Artist, and American Consul at Rome, on his departure for Italy.

Embodied music lives,—
Sculptured to life the forms appear,
And pictured verse deceives !
Yes, Poet-Painter, though no words
Ring through thy witchery,
A deeper spell thine Art affords,
In silent poetry !
The pencil, chisel, harp, and pen
Are different tongues alone ;
The same high truths they preach to men,
One parent source they own :
The same sweet eyes that shone each night
On Byron's boyhood dream,
In Guido's worship glassed their light,
And gave his pencil's theme ;
'Round Chantry's couch their beauty hung,
And circled wild Mozart,—
The same inspirers, ever young,—
The Auroras of the heart !

IV.

Then on, my friend, with faith and hope !
A starry road you tread.

Right onward, upward,—boldly cope
  The Dead who are not dead!
Soon for the clime of song and art,—
  The fountain school of Fame,—
Your earnest spirit will depart,
  A pilgrim's draught to claim.
Go proudly onward,—strive and try,—
  Invoke the Masters' spell,—
The priests of art,—the prophets high,
  Round Valambrosa's well.
These on thy pencil will bestow
  Their colorings rich and strange,
And warm thy fancy with the glow,
  That bids the canvass—Change!
Drink at the fount, and then return
  Home to thy land afar,
And here reveal the Muses' urn,
  Beneath the forest star:
And though the Arts,—the flowery Arts,—
  As yet have scarce a home
Within our borders, there are hearts
  Shall hail you when you come;
And this young land of Freedom's Faith
  Again rejoice to see

A son of hers bear back a wreath
  From sunny Italy.
Then boldly on ! keep aye in view
  The pictured cliffs of Fame,
And thine, it may be to renew
  All but an ALLSTON'S name !

THE NEW GENESIS;

OR,

THE CREATION OF THE ELEMENTS.

A Rabbinical Tradition.

"In the beginning,"—ere the Earth
Was rounded into form and place,
Before the starry worlds had birth,
Or man was formed in life and grace,
When all was "void and shapeless,"—GOD—
Of life, the uncreated source,
His chosen angel sent abroad,
To vivify the Universe.
Swift, from the spirit walls of heaven,
The sweet apostle sped her flight,—
YOUNG NATURE,—unto whom was given,
A portion of the Almighty's might.
Far through the boundless space her coming shone,
Like the faint blushes of some rosy dawn!

Suspended in unpillar'd space,
With floating angels all around,

The fair enchantress paused apace,
  And spoke with voice of trumpet sound :
" Here ! build we here : The temples high,
  The palaces and halls of life,—
The archictecture of the sky,—
  The world with strength and beauty rife.—
Let there be AIR !"—And, as she spoke,
  She breathed afar a vital spell,
That all the senseless void awoke,
  And filled its vast receptacle : —
Clear crystal walls transparent sprang on high,
And suns, and stars, and rainbows decked the sky.

Smiling divinely on the scene,
  The beauteous angel waved her hand,
And bade, with proud celestial mien,
  Appear the solid earth and land !
Low rumbling thunder rolled below,
  As ether into substance fled,
And, bounding, with a giant throe,
  The EARTH upon her orbit sped.
The caverns vast, the mountains high,
  The plains and vales in verdure drest,
The waving woods,—swept proudly by,

Upon her vast majestic breast.
The angels gazed with pleasure and surprise,
As the new wonder met their starry eyes!

But, half-unformed, remained the Earth,
Until the legate of the skies
Bade seas and oceans usher forth,
And gushing rills and rivers rise.
"Let WATER be!"—and, at the word,
The liquid element appears,—
The thundering cataract is heard,—
The crystal fount, the desert cheers!
Weltering around, like molten glass,
The vast interminable waves,
The solid continents, embrace,—
And fill with floods the ocean caves.
Iow beautiful to angel visions, then,
The destined homes of uncreated men!

"Earth is complete," the angel said,
"But oh, how cold!"—and, quick as thought,
A glittering shaft of lightning sped,
Which by a mountain's peak was caught.
The broad volcano glared around,—

A gleaming pharos lit the sky,—
The burning lava scorched the ground,
And woods and forests flamed on high.
The angel waved her hand and stayed
The conflagration in its birth,—
And soon the restless FIRE she made
Assume its destined place on earth !
To each and all, by sweet creative art,
Climates and seasons, she bestowed their part.

'Earth is complete," she now began,
" The work of goodness is fulfilled,"
The ELEMENTS are framed for man,
As by the Almighty Ruler willed.
Oh, may Man value them aright,
And heed the lesson that they give,
In LOVE and FRIENDSHIP to delight,
In Peace and CHARITY to live !
These are the laws by NATURE given,—
The precious mandates of the skies,—
They'll shed on earth the light of heaven,
And make a second Paradise !
" Farewell !" she said, and, with her angel guard,
Once more to heaven's high home in joy repaired !

THE STONE MOUNTAIN,

GEORGIA.*

Stupendous Thought in Nature's mind !
  Some night-mare Dream!—some gaunt Despair!
What frantic passions were combined,
  Vast Incubus ! to shape thee there ;
Volcanic shudders shook the wind
  As thou wert laid all bleak and bare !
No wilder woes were ever wrought
Than in thy birth—Titanic Thought !

All palpable thou loomest now,
  Strange massive Miracle of Stone !
The fierce storms sweep thy bald, huge brow,—
  The sunlight sees thee there alone !
Far 'round, the vales, beneath thee bow,
  The tall trees at thy feet are strewn.

---

* This immense solitary peak of solid rock, in De Kalb county, Georgia, about 12 miles from Atlanta, near the Railroad to Augusta, is three thousand feet in height, and over six miles in circumference at its base. It is a huge conical hemisphere, with a precipitous declivity of nearly a thousand feet on its northern side.

Man's mightiest pyramids, to thee,
Are paltry bubbles on the sea!

Northward, in one sheer precipice,
  Thy giant form lifts to the sky;
So high, so steep, so grim it is,
  It shrinks the boldest gazer's eye;
And 'round its far extremities,
  The dizzied eagle scarce can fly.
Yon boulder from its verge displace,—
'Tis crushed to powder at thy base!

Imperishable in thy might,
  Thou there hast stood from earliest time;
The rocking centuries, in their flight,
  Still saw thee changeless and sublime;
Mute harmonist! while day and night
  Kept on their old perpetual rhyme!
Earth's empires all, like shadows, run,
Thou art cöeval with the sun!

Well might the wild man of the Land—
  The buskined Warrior of the Wood—

Deem thee an Altar, vast and grand,
  For demons fierce or spirits good.
By night, he saw weird shadows stand
  Upon thy loftiest solitude ;
Wild sounds come howling down thy side,
While wilder tones from heaven replied !

As beat the thunder on thy brow,
  And arrowy lightnings 'round it played,
He saw Manito's great *Pow-wow*,
  And demon forms in strife arrayed:
Or, when the Rainbow's roseate glow,
  A halo 'round thy forehead made,
Fair forms he saw, with wings of white,
Flash radiant in the evening light !

In later years when war and strife
  Drove maddening through the crimsoned dells,
He fled, for safety and for life,
  To thy high cliffs and rocky swells ;
There, fortressed well with child and wife
  Amid his tribe, secure he dwells.
No foe can scale the winding way,
Where fierce *Muscogee* stands at bay !

Sad tales of softness and of love,
  Old legends tell, of thy career ;
How from the *Red Hawk* fled the *Dove*,
  And sought a sanctuary here :
No safe-guard did thy summit prove,
  And, driven by anguish, hate and fear,
From thy dread peak she leaped afar,—
Her white-robes like a falling star !

At night her faint scream oft is heard,
  Some moonlight night, when all is still,—
Or is't the shriek of boding bird,
  Or cry of panther from the hill ?
I fain believe tradition's word,
  Tis "*Ona-chopa pelen-chil.*"
Thus, though the tribes have passed away,
Their fond romances with us stay !

Grim Mount of Stone !—one summer's morn,
  Upon thy loftiest height I stood,
And, far away, o'er hill and lawn,
  O'er pictured town, and sea-like wood,
And streams, like silvery serpents, drawn,—
  A boundless landscape, 'round me viewed !

Earth seemed to swim in light below,—
Fair Georgia, in transcendent glow!

Long shall my mind, that hour recall,—
  That glorious view,—that wild weird Height,—
The thoughts that kept my soul in thrall,
  As with some spell of magic might:
For there, to memory's eye, came all
  The Red Tribes, vanished long from sight,
And hailed thee, vast Memorial Stone,
As Nature's Tribute to her Children gone!

BALAKLAVA.

Oh, the Charge at Balaklava !
  Oh, that rash and fatal Charge !
Never was a fiercer, braver,
Than that Charge at Balaklava,
  On the battle's bloody marge !
All the day, the Russian columns,—
  Fortress huge, and blazing banks,—
Poured their dread destructive volumes
  On the French and English ranks—
  On the gallant allied ranks !
Earth and sky seemed rent asunder
By the loud incessant thunder !
When a strange, but stern command,—
Needless, heedless, rash command,—
Came to Nolan's little band,—
Scarce six hundred men and horses
Of those vast contending forces,—
" England's lost ! oh, charge and save her—
Charge the pass of Balaklava !"
        Oh, that rash and fatal charge,
        On the battle's bloody marge !

Far away the Russian Eagles
  Soar o'er smoking hill and dell,
And their hordes, like howling beagles,
  Dense and countless, 'round them yell!
Thundering cannon, deadly mortar
Sweep the field on every quarter!
Never, since the days of Jesus,
Trembled so the Chersonesus!
  Here behold the Gallic Lillies,—
  Stout St. Louis' golden Lillies!—
  Float as erst at old Ramillies!—
  And, beside them, lo! the Lion,—
  England's proud unconquered Lion!—
  With her trophied Cross, is flying.
Glorious standards! shall they waver
On the field of Balaklava?
No, by heavens! at that command,—
Sudden, rash, but stern command,—
Charges Nolan's little band!
    Brave Six Hundred! lo! they charge
    On the battle's bloody marge!

Down yon deep and skirted valley,
  Where the crowded cannon play,—

Where the Czar's fierce cohorts rally,
Cossack, Kalmuck, savage Kalli,—
Down that gorge they sweep away !
Down that new Thermopylæ,
Flashing swords and helmets, see !
Underneath the iron shower,
To the brazen cannon's jaws,
Heedless of their deadly power,
Press they without fear or pause,—
To the very cannon's jaws !
Gallant Nolan, brave as Roland
At the field of Roncesvalles,
Dashes down the fatal valley,
Dashes on the bolt of death,
Shouting with his latest breath,
"Charge them, gallants ! do not waver,
Charge the pass of Balaklava !"
Oh, that rash and fatal Charge,
On the battle's bloody marge !

Now the bolts of vollied thunder
Rend that little band asunder.
Steed and rider wildly screaming,

Screaming wildly, sink away,—
Late so proudly, proudly gleaming.
Now but lifeless clods of clay,—
Now but bleeding clods of clay ;
Never since the days of Jesus,
Saw such sight, the Chersonesus !
Yet your remnant, brave Six Hundred,
Presses onward, onward, onward.
Till they storm the bloody pass,—
Till, like brave Leonidas,
They storm the deadly pass !
Sabering Cossack, Kalmuck, Kalli,
In that wild shot-rended valley,—
Drenched with fire and blood, like lava,
Awful pass of Balaklava !
Oh, that rash and fatal Charge,
On the battle's bloody marge !

For now Russia's rallied forces,—
Swarming hordes of Cossack horses,
Trampling o'er the reeking corses,—
Drive the thinned assailants back,
Drive the feeble remnant back !
O'er their late heroic track !

Vain, alas ! Now rent and sundered,
Vain your struggles, brave Six Hundred !
Half your numbers lie asleep,
In that valley dark and deep.
Weak and wounded you retire
From that hurricane of fire,—
That tempestuous storm of fire !
But no soldiers, firmer, braver,
  Ever trod a field of fame,
Than the Knights of Balaklava,—
  Honor to each hero's name !
Yet their country long shall mourn
For her ranks so rashly shorn,—
So gallantly but madly shorn,
          In that fierce and fatal Charge,
          On the battle's bloody marge.

NATURE'S LESSON.

The face of Nature lives with beauty,
  But man neglects the bright display ;
All-unobservant of his duty,
  He wiles a sightless life away !

How sweet the rosy morning breaking
  O'er dewy lawn and wooded hill !—
Fair alchemist !—all-golden making
  The waving grove, the rimpling rill !

Goes with the sun imperial splendor
  O'er sea and sky and festal earth ;
From blue-browed noon to twilight tender,
  Each way, are orbs of heavenly birth !

When far away, 'mid flashing banners,—
  A countless army,—sinks the sun,
What watch-fires light the blue savannahs,
  With spirit-guards 'round every one !

All through the night, they burn and brighten—
The out-posts of the heavenly land,—
Beneath their rays the hill-tops whiten,
And still as spell-bound giants stand!

And oh the moon!—pale mother Mary!—
How fair *she* makes the balmy night!—
Her brow may wane, her beauty vary,
Through all her presence is delight!

Yes, ever lovely!—earth and ocean
Feel fairer in her silvery beam:—
The swan of heaven!—with stateliest motion
She cleaves her blue star-pebbled stream!

Lo! like an arch by angels bended,
For triumph high in Spirit Land,
Enwreathed with flowers all-hued and blended,
The rainbow o'er the valley spanned!

Almost, it seems, with beauty vital;
The valley glows 'neath its embrace;
And yon clear stream, with proud requital,
Slides through its deeply mirrored grace,

All things around thus tell of Eden,
  If man would only list and look ;
All have a beauty, art exceeding,
  From sunset's pomp to crystal brook.

The Seasons,—each a new creation,—
  In linked circles press around ;
"Let there be light !"—the revelation
  Responsive clothes the quickened ground

When Spring o'er hill and dell is blushing,—
  A country girl all smiles and flowers,—
What constant melody is gushing
  From countless minstrels through the bowers!

The crimson Summer has his glory,
  And mellow Autumn rainbow light,—
And Winter, Lear-like, all hoary,
  Sparkles with gems and robes of white !

These things are given us to inspire
  A love for Nature's gentle face ;
To make man grateful and admire
  His beauty-builded dwelling-place.

Oh yes! if we would listen to it,
  The anthem 'round, below, above,
Each heart would leap to life—a poet!—
  Each soul be brimmed with bliss and love!

For I have learned these pregnant lessons,—
  The soul is fashioned by the spheres,—
Imperishable in its essence,
  It still the stamp of Nature wears!

By beauty into beauty moulded,
  Or marred by blackness and by storm,
From influences which enfold it,
  It takes its coloring, and its form.

Who then would perfect strength inherit,
  Must feed his soul at Beauty's fount—
The breast of Nature,—and his spirit, soo
  In triumph, thence, will starward mount.

THE DEATH OF JACKSON.

A wail of woe through all the land !
  A stricken nation's plaintive cry !
Sackcloth and gloom on every hand !
  A shadow o'er the sunny sky !
The muffled drum, the tolling bell,
  The 'plaining bugle's sinking breath,
The booming cannon's sudden swell,—
  All speak thy presence, mighty Death !
Yes ! see the star-wreathed eagle stoops,
  And in the darkness folds his wing ;
And lo ! yon lordly banner droops,
  That never vailed before a king !
Oh ! why this heavy grief and gloom ?
  And why this sudden, sad eclipse !
Ah ! list—the plaintive answers come,
  In sobbing tones, from freedom's lips—
Columbia's stricken children mourn
A chief and prophet from their altars torn !

Well may ye weep ! Columbia's sons,
  Of every creed and party weep !
For never, from your treasured ones,

A nobler soul has sunk to sleep.
Your country's latest boast and pride ;
His fame has spread o'er all the world,
And poured her glory's starry tide
Where'er her banners were unfurled.
The nations of each distant clime
Have learned to breathe his mighty name ;
And scholar's scroll, and minstrel's rhyme,
Have wed it to immortal fame ;
Such spirits are a nation's stars—
Without them, history were dark ;
And oh ! amid life's ocean jars,
Would perish freedom's fragile bark !
Then weep with tides of deepest grief,
The hero, patriot, statesman, sage, and chief !

Wail for the Warrior of the West !
Who, in your country's morning hour,
Though but a boy, exposed his breast
To shield her from a tyrant's power.
Ah ! see his fair and silken curls
Stained with the crimson current's hue !
Yet bravely still his arm unfurls
The struggling standard of the few !

Years pass ; and, by deep forest streams,
  He quells a savage foeman's power ;
Till, through the trees, the genial beams
  Of peace dispense their golden shower !
Again, by Mississippi's wave,
  He sees our olden foemen pour ;
But ever bold and prompt to save,
  He hurls the Titans from the shore ;
Then weep your mightiest warrior dead,
Who thrice your country saved from hostile tread !

But now the sage and statesman mourn !
  For he was great in peace as war ;
And laurel-wreaths his brow adorn,
  More bright than Victory's crimson star ;
In vision keen, in judgement sound,
  In honest effort ever true,
In knowledge of the heart profound,
  An inspiration thence he drew.
His country owned his sterling worth,
  And placed him in her chosen seat,
Above the loftiest thrones of earth—
  With tyrants crouching at his feet !
Nobly he filled his kingly sphere ;

And ever, like the olden sage,
Led on his countrymen to share
The treasures of the promised age!
Then mourn, oh! reft and widowed land,
The latest ruler, of thine early band!

Yes, freemen, mourn! but 'midst the gloom,
Your grief and darkness to assuage,
Turn back your eyes, and view yon room
Within his own loved Hermitage!
The sunset of a Sabbath eve
Shines round that couch with golden glow,
And o'er the kneeling forms that grieve,
And 'round that head as white as snow!
Ah! seems he not some prophet old,
Just lingering on the brink of time?
And hark! what scenes his lips unfold
Of pleasures in the blessed clime!
The sun sinks low;—athwart his beam
A glimpse of "wheels and horses" given!
Was it a shadow or a dream?
Elijah has gone up to heaven!
Then mourn! but, "not as if in vain;"
His memory, like a mantle, shall remain!

THE DOUBLE DREAM.

"Our life is two-fold."—*Byron.*

Fondly all through yesternight,
  Fondly did I dream of thee,
And my soul, in deep delight,
  Wandered with thine far and free :
Brightest visions round me shone ;
  All for which my heart had yearned,
All the dearest scenes I'd known,
  'Neath the spell of sleep, returned :
Fancy too assumed the helm,
  And the ship of thought drove far,
O'er the dream-sea's mystic realm,—
  Thou, the sole and guiding star !
Wilt thou hear me sing the scenes
  Mirrored in that Eden sleep ?—
Unto thee my spirit leans,
  Enchantress, for the meaning deep !

I.

First, within a brilliant hall,
  'Mid the youthful, gay, and bright,

Glanced a form more fair than all,
  Like a spirit on my sight!
Proudly through the circling dance,
  As, between the stars, the moon,
Moved she, with a stately glance,
  To the old and festive tune.
Sweet the music,—for it seemed
  But her motion's atmosphere,—
Filled with light that round her beamed,—
  Captivating eye and ear.
Thoughts, like fountains years-subdued,
  In my bosom poured their tide,
And, entranced like Saul, I stood,
  Mute with homage, at her side!

II.

Months seemed passed,—and now a scene,
  Pastoral-sweet, was round me spread :—
On the hills, the spring-time's green,
  And the blue sky overhead!
Winding down a forest river,
  In a lightly leaning boat—
Snowy sails in breezy quiver,—
  By her side I seemed to float.

Music from her voice was breathed,
  Sweeter than a singing bird's ;
Smiles around her lips were wreathed,
  Like the starlight of her words.
Long we sailed,—and passion's sighs,
  Kneeling then, I dared to pour,—
But a storm o'erwhelmed the skies !
  I was wrecked upon the shore !

III.

Fancy now more wild became !
  Far through foreign lands I roved,
Armed,—a knight,—in lists of fame,
  Championing my Ladye-Love.
Pomp and splendor round me shone,
  Cavaliers and maidens bright,—
But above them all was one
  Beautiful as morning light !—
On my shield her scroll I bore,—
  FAIREST VIRGIN OF THE WEST,—
Round my breast her scarf I wore,
  And her colors on my crest.
Shouting loud defiance out,

Sought I then the marshalled strife,—
Proudly with the boldest fought,—
Perilling with joy my life!
Soon a victor, from the scene,
To her feet I bore the prize,—
Crowned her there as Beauty's Queen,—
Drank my plaudits from her eyes!

IV.

But a change now strangely passed
O'er my wild and fevered dream;—
Where tall trees their shadows cast,
By a sweet, secluded stream,
We were roving;—overhead,
Smiling like an angel's face,
Hung the moon, as if to shed
Love-light on that trysting place.
In the shadows and the hush
Of that old, moon-silvered grove,—
Prayer, and vow, and tear, and blush!—
Plighted we our troth and love!—
What beside this then occurred
Underneath that smiling sky,

Thou must ask that startled bird !—
  Thou must dream as well as I !

Such my visions yesternight,—
  So my spirit roved with thine,—
Drinking in a wild delight,—
  Revelling 'mid scenes divine !
Strange indeed our dreams are wrought ;
  Fancy, Memory, and Hope,
All combine to cheat the thought
  With their gay kaleidoscope !
What within *my* dream was drawn
  From the Past, thy heart can tell ;
What was Fancy's work alone,
  Thou canst see and solve as well.
But our dreams are Sybil's too ;—
  Could we read their visits right,
We might in their lessons view
  Stars to guide the Future's night.
Then, Enchantress, solve the scenes
  Mirrored in my last night's sleep !
Unto thee my spirit leans,
  Belshazzar-like, for meaning deep.

THE DEATH OF RICHARD HENRY WILDE.

The harp that sang "the Summer Rose,"
In strains, so sweetly and so well,
That, soft as dews at evening's close,
The pure and liquid numbers fell,
Is hushed and shattered ! now, no more
Its silvery chords their music pour ;
But, crushed by an untimely blow,
Both harp and flower in dust lie low !

The bard !—alas, I knew him well !
A noble, generous, gentle, heart,
Which, as his brave hand struck the shell
Poured feeling through the veins of Art.
What radiant beauty 'round his lyre !—
Pure as his loved Italian fire !—
He caught the sweetest beams of rhyme,—
The Tasso of our Western clime !

Nor this alone : a loftier power,
That shone in halls of High Decree,

And swayed the feelings of the hour,
  As summer winds, the rippled sea,—
Bright eloquence! to him was given:
The spark, the Prophet drew from heaven!
It touched his lips with patriot flame,
And shed a halo 'round his name!

As late I saw, I see him now!
  His stalwart form, his graceful mien,
His long, white locks, his smiling brow,
  His eyes benignant and serene!
How pleasant 'round the social hearth,
When listening to his tones of mirth!
What lessons of the good and true,
The brave, the beautiful, he drew!

Droop down thy willows, Southern land!
  Thy bard, thine orator is dead.
He sleeps where broad magnolias stand,
  With "Summer roses" o'er his head!
The lordly River, sweeping by,
Curves 'round his grave, with solemn sigh,
And, from yon twinkling orange stem,
The "Mock-Bird" pours his requiem!

Bard of the South !—the " Summer Rose "
  May perish with the " Autumn leaf, "
The " footprints left on Tampa's " shores
  May vanish with a date as brief :
But thine shall be the " life " of fame ;
No winter winds can wreck thy name ;
And future minstrels shall rehearse
Thy virtues, in memorial verse !

TO A FAIR VIRGINIAN.

Birth-Day Verses.

Fair daughter of Virginia !— the Autumn months again
Have, 'mid their yellow sunshine their foliage, fruit and grain,
Brought back the happy morning, when to the smilling skies,
Like young and dewy blossoms, first oped thine infant eyes ;
When friends in joyous greeting, stood 'round with smile and tear,
And hailed the cradled beauty, as a missioned Angel here;
And now when bright fulfilment has crowned those early dreams,
And again thy natal planet in diamond beauty beams,
I too would bring a tribute for one so fair and sweet,
And strew a poet's blessings, like flowers, beneath thy feet !

Sweet daughter of Virginia !—a noblė birth was thine,
And proud ancestral graces, in thy young glances, shine;

The blood of Pocahontas !—the forest bride and queen,
Her strong but gentle spirit, her soft but stately mien !
The genius of thy mother !—whose tender minstrel lay
Shed, o'er the Old Dominion, its sunniest golden ray !—
The virtues of thy sisters, so beautiful and bright,
Whose minds are crystal fountains that overflow with light !
All these were sweet influences, to elevate thy heart,
And mould thee in thy loveliness, to fill a perfect part !

Blest daughter of Virginia !—thy life thus far has been
But as some gentle river that flows through banks of green !
The blue sky bending brightly within the dimpled wave.
And flower-eyes overleaning, their pictured lids to lave ;
Fair birds with glancing pinions, bright barques with freighted sweets,
And song, and laugh, and echo, from circling, green retreats !—
These emblem thy fair girlhood ; and heaven grant that they
May, with increasing beauty, shine 'round thine after way !—

And when thy life's bright current shall with another's
blend,
May both pass on as sweetly, in Paradise to end!

Kind daughter of Virginia!—few days I've known thee
here,
Yet, like redoubled sunshine, they've made thee loved
and dear.
I love thee for thy beauty, thine innocence and truth,
Thy frank, confiding spirit, thy mind so bright in youth.
For though a lonely stranger, from friends and home afar,
Thy smiles have lit my pathway, like the beauty of a star!
Then long as memory liveth, I shall recall with pride,
The fond and joyous moments I've lingered by thy side;
And ever on thy birth-day, my heart and harp would
twine
The roses of affection to decorate thy shrine!

TWO YEARS AGO.

Two years ago, Medora, I pledged my love to thee,
By all life's fondest visions, and my soul's integrity ;
And thy gentle heart responded to the echoes of my own,
And, like a wind-touched instrument, gave back affection's
tone !

Two years ago, Medora, in the soft moonlighted breeze,
That swayed the dappled shadows beneath the cedar trees,
What rapture, and what visions made either bosom warm,
As, with lips in love united, I pressed thy trembling form !

Two years ago, Medora, I breathed a sad farewell,
In those grouped and silent cedars, and the moon that
'round us fell ;
But we plighted vow and token,—" Fidelity through
pain."
Ah ! dost thou not remember the ring we broke in twain ?

Two years have passed, Medora, and again my heart has
come,
Like the worn and weary Hebrew, to his early nopes and
home,
But I find thee strangely altered, those trysting scenes
forgot,
That ring changed for another's, those vows remembered
not !

Two years ! two years ! Medora,—is this the life of love ?
Its winged and silver circle, the shortest star's above ?
Are breeze, and beam, and shadow, the emblems of its
stay ?
And Hope, and Faith, and Feeling, the dreams of
yesterday ?

Two years ! alas, Medora ! I write the words with pain,—
The epitaph of passion !—inscribed upon my brain !
Well, read, and scorn the lesson !—thy new love strive
to please,
But thy heart shall weep hereafter for those moonlit
cedar trees.

MY MOTHER.

My mother !—at that dear and sacred word,
What thoughts, deep-treasured in this breast, are stirr'd:
How speeds my heart back to long vanished hours,
When life was sunshine, o'er a path of flowers !—
When the young spirit, like an April bird,
Poured forth glad music, in each sinless word !
Boyhood's lost Eden, at that mention, beams,
Its curving sky,—its clear and laughing streams ;—
Its hopes, its pleasures—fancies and its fears,
Its wild ambitionings—its easy tears,
All—all arise, like stars at even-time,
And shed their softness on my manhood's prime !
I see each favorite spot, where then I roved,—
The foes I hated, and the friends I loved !
My morning sports, sweet, innocent and pure,—
My sunset rambles by the river's shore,
Like dreams, return,—and oh, more dear than these,
My night-time worship, at my mother's knees !—
When she, as low my faltering prayers I said,
Invoked heaven's blessings on her first-born's head !

Mother !—dear mother !—though my heart hath grown,
As manhood's will, by care, well nigh to stone,—
Though with a cold, indifferent eye, I gaze
On the fair scenes, that charmed my earlier days,—
And scarce a joy, that, flower-like, wreathed my heart,
In life's young morn, hath, in its noon, a part,—
Though the dear friends, I loved so fondly then,
Have left my side, or grown to cold-browed men,—
And I now mingle in life's fever-fray,
With little lingering of that better day,—
Yet still, my mother, unto thee my breast
Turns, as the ark-dove, to its only rest,
And finds its hopes, affections, feelings, there,
Mirrored in kindness, unestranged by care,—
Twines round thy bosom, as the vine that clings
Around the oak, from which its nurture springs,—
And unto thee, its filial worship gives,
As e'er it will, whilst its pulsation lives,
With a devotion fonder, deeper far,
Than the rapt Chaldean pays his idol star !

Yes ! dearest mother !—thongh mine eyes have seen
Full many a brow, as fair as Paphia's queen,—

Though oft, bewildered, I have gazed on forms
Would madden seraphs, with their starry charms,—
And felt their influence o'er my feelings reign,
Like night's pale maiden, o'er the restless main,—
Yet still, my mother, I have never found
One who could claim affections so profound,—
So free from selfishness,—so pure and strong,—
As *these*, which ever unto thee belong.
Thy high, pale brow, —thy soft and tender eye,—
Thy gentle smile,—thy dear maternal sigh,—
Thy changeless love,—are dearer far, to me,
Than fame's bright baubles are, or e'er can be !—
I would not give one kindly word of thine,
For all the music poured at Beauty's shrine !
And oh ! when life's last pulses cease to play,
And all its dreams, like eve-clouds, melt away,—
Upon my heart, undimmed by time or care,
Thy name will stand, MY MOTHER !—written there!

1844.

A SOLDIER'S LOVE DREAM.

Tampa Bay Florida.

Behold yon star !—how soft its ray
Melts over Tampa's cradled bay !
How brightly, on the waters blue,
It's mellow gold-beams fling their hue,
And, shimmering softly, sink and shine
Far down in ocean's crystal shrine !
  Mid pearls and corals glistening bright—
    Mid crimson shells and sea-gems rare,—
  That star reflected meets the sight,
    And glimmers, like a diamond, there !—
Until the wanderer's gazing eyes,
In fondness, seek its native skies !

That star, fair girl, is like to thee,—
Enshrined in love and purity !—
It's calm, clear lustre, all thine own,
When last upon my path you shone !—
And now, like it, o'er Memory's lake,
Thy heavenly beauties gently break ;

And deep, in fond affection's shrine,
Mid ruder thoughts,—mid grief and care,—
Thy starry virtues, lingering, shine,
And glimmer, like a diamond, there !—
Until my fond, but wayward mind,
Reverts to her I left behind !

Yes,—though my footsteps now have gone
Far, far from thee, beloved one ;
Though now no more thine eyes' dark light
Gleams on my heart, so calm and bright ;
And thy dear voice no more is heard,
Breathing sweet music in each word ;
Nor more thy clear and sunny smile,—
Thy tossing curls,—thy playful lip,—
Thy gentle looks, devoid of guile,—
Bless me with their companionship !—
Yet, still, remembrance of thy charms
Lives in my breast, and grief disarms ;
And, like those star-beams on yon bay,
Casts lustre on my lonely way !

And now, though mountains intervene,
And ocean spreads his waves between,—

Though toil and strife are 'round me here,
And "war's red banners flout the air,"—
I turn awhile from them away,
And dedicate to thee this lay,—
To thee, whose young and sinless heart,
Is Virtue's own peculiar shrine,—
Where Love and Genius grace impart,
And Beauty's lustres softly shine.—
To thee,—my light,—my life,—my star!
Whose radiance glimmers from afar,
O'er mount, and plain and heaving sea,
And fills my breast with thoughts of thee!

A MONODY.

And thou art dead!—alas, young, eagle-hearted
  Friend of my youth, thy bright career is o'er!
From earth, thy joyous spirit has departed,
  And I shall see thy manly form no more!
No more shall press thy hand, or hear thy voice
Ring out, in eloquence, o'er earthly joys!

Thy lip is stilled—dust on thy stainless forehead!
  Thine eye is dimmed beneath its snowy lid!
Thy mind, that seemed a light from heaven borrowed,
  Like an extinguished lamp, in death lies hid—
Gone from life's sorrows, pleasures, hopes, and fears,
And naught is left of thee, but memory and tears!

I knew it was man's lot, to early perish,
    But did not dream that in life's morning bloom,
Thou—whom all hearts did love to joy and cherish—
  Wouldst meet the stern, irrevocable doom!
I thought I saw, in thee, a spirit sent
To bless and cheer our darkened firmament!

Oft by thy side, at morning's freshening prime,
  Or when calm eve was crimsoning the sky,
Bright scenes I pictured, of thy coming time,
  Bright as the prospects then before the eye!
Hope too was thine, and in thy heart was stirred
Her mild, sweet music, like a spring-time bird!

How vain are man's opinions—futile—frail!
  His hopes as transient as a meteor's flash—
His life as fleeting as a school-boy's tale—
  To dust, his proudest trophies, death can dash!
Thus, in a moment, o'er thy path was thrown
  Fell blight—and all thy promise withered—gone!

As falls, in Spring, the young and laughing blossom—
  As sinks the eagle from his sky career—
As dies a vain hope in an infant's bosom—
  As sudden falls the arrow-stricken deer—
So was thy pinion broken, and thy heart
Stilled in its pulse, by an untimely dart!

Far from thy home, thy fond and tender mother—
  From thy young sister's gentle watchings, far—

Who oft, in memory of their distant brother,
  Blessed the low twinklings of the Southern star—
In a strange land, with strangers 'round thy bed,
Thy noble spirit, from life's commune, fled !

Yet friends were 'round thee, in that darkening hour—
  The good have always friends where'er they go !—
Who would have saved thee, gladly, from that Power,
  Whose touch is misery, and whose breath is woe.
They saw thy grief—they vainly tried to save—
They closed thine eyes—they heaped thine early grave !

And o'er the spot, where now thy form reposes,
  Will wandering Friendship shed the frequent tear—
Young maiden hands will deck its turf with roses,
  And manly bosoms leave their tributes there !
No gift more fitting, can I, for thee, bring,—
This humble flower is all my offering.

OLYMPIC SPORTS.

A Prize Address.

In classic days, when mythologic Greece
Filled her broad temples with the arts of peace ;
When Learning flourished, and when Thought sublime
Framed Miracles, as lovely as her clime ;
When Sculpture—the Prometheus of New Life,—
With Nature vied, in proud creative strife ;
When Painting brightened in her Iris hues,
And deathless Music wed the Lyric Muse ;
When life seemed all a golden holiday,
And man, a reveller in pleasure's ray ;—
Then Genius rose, to hold a Festal Court,
And grouped these splendors for Olympic Sport !

Proud on her plains, the Attic Circle spread,
Where all the Muses were for contest led.
There the strong *athlete* showed his wondrous powers,
While the gay *mimic* cheered the frolic hours ;
Swift o'er the field the gallant coursers run,
Till steed and rider seem to be but one ;

Far rings the shout—the echo of renown,—
And the proud victor wears the Olive Crown !

In later days, when Rome—imperial Queen,—
On on all her seven hills, in pomp was seen,—
Her stateliest palaces, with classic names,
Were shrines devoted to the Public Games !
Lo ! on yon mount, the Coliseum view,—
Art's proudest monument—the City's too !
What countless thousands crowd its collonades !—
What thrilling sports, processions, and parades !
The loftiest noble, with the Wrestler vies,—
The gay Gymnast around th' arena flies,—
The imprisoned Swordsmen join in mortal fray,—
And die, " to make a Roman Holiday !"

Such times are gone ; but we, with kindred powers,
Would seek once more the famed Olympian bowers.
Upon this spot, whose crumbling ruins tell
How late, by fire, a sculptured palace fell,—
Our city's boast and pride !—we come to rear
A shrine for mirth,—a Roman temple here !
Around this broad arena, you shall see
The flying steed, in native majesty ;

The gallant Barb will skim along this plain,
As o'er his free-born deserts once again ;
The Tartar, too, will spurn the hurrying ground,
With wild Mazeppa still upon him bound !
While from the West, the Indian's steed shall come,
Fierce with the impulse of his battle drum !

But, chief of all, here man shall move in pride,
And show how grace and strength may be allied.
Lo ! now behold him stand, like Hercules,
Wielding his giant club with infant ease !
Now, like Apollo, see his faultless form,
In every flexile shape, still glowing warm !
And now, like Mercury, with wingéd feet,
He tiptoe stands upon his courser fleet !
Fair Woman, too, with wild, bewitching grace,
Joins, like Camilla, in the circling race ;
While, from each kindling eye, and glowing cheek ;
The deep emotions to the gazer speak.—
Thus every phase of life we seek to show,
And join the arts of Garrick and Ducrow !

Nor this alone ; here Momus holds his court,
And Wit and Folly keep perpetual sport.

Fools are abundant in this world's wide bowers ;
But where—where will you find such fools as ours ?
Not the buffoon, who, with his stupid laugh
At sensless *bulls*, but proves himself a *calf ;*
Nor the dull clodpole, who with *thread-bare* jokes,
Shows his own—folly, to the wondering folks ;
But fools of that renowned and gifted kind,
Whom Shakespeare fashioned in his Pantheon mind!
Whose sparkling humor flows with Champagne cheer,
And is not kept and bottled, *like small beer !*
Such, with our well-known Ethiopian Band,—
With Smith—yes, famous *John Smith*—in command,
Must gain loud plaudits from the hands I view,
Or they must yield " the bells and cap " to you !

Patrons and Friends! Bright eyes around this Ring—
Lips red with beauty, like young flowers in spring,—
Our greeting's o'er ! To you we now confide
The feats and follies which we shall provide;
If you approve, these walls ere long shall rise,
In loftier grandeur, to these sunny skies,—
And this Arena prove a loved resort,
The choicest temple of Olympic Sport !

THE DUCHESS OF DEVONSHIRE.*

Bold Painter, try thy utmost skill!
In vain thy heart, in vain thy will!
Thou canst not paint that brow so fair—
Its fondling curls of shining hair!
Thy pallette hath no tints can vie
With the rich radiance of that eye!
Nor picture forth the beams that speak
From the clear sunshine of that cheek,
Where snow and coral intertwine
To consecrate for love a shrine!
And oh, 'twill all thy art eclipse,
    And make thee throw thy pencil by—
    Though tinted from the sunset sky,—
To paint the elysium of those lips!

---

* "Gainsborough, the rival of Sir Joshua Reynolds, in vain attempted to paint the portrait of Georgiana Spencer, the celebrated Duchess of Devonshire. She was then in the full bloom of her youth, and her charms and conversation took away that readiness of hand and happiness of touch which belonged to the painter in his ordinary moments. The portrait was so little to his satisfaction that he refused to send it to Chatworth. Drawing his wet pencil across a mouth, which all who saw it thought exquisitely beautiful, he said, 'Her Grace is too hard for me.'"

Enthusiast ! hast thou ever seen
  The glorious forms of Grecian art,—
The statue of the Egyptian Queen,—
  The Goddess of the trembling heart ?
Hast thou e'er gazed on the sublime
Forms of Italia's classic clime,—
Where, as the ancient minstrels tell,
The stars of heaven came down to dwell,
With all the lustre of the skies
Around them still, and in their eyes,
And, finding there no fitter shine,
Took woman's form, and made 't divine ?
If thou hast ever gazed on these
Earth-bound, but heaven-born Pleiades,
And on thy canvas learned to trace,
Raphael-like, their forms of grace,
  In all their peerless purity,
Then mayst thou paint, and not before,
The Loveliness which all adore,—
  This new Divinity !

Oh, if Apelles, when of old
  He stood before Campaspe bright,

With hand as skilled and heart as bold
  As ever drew a form of light,
Found all his art in vain, and threw
  Himself in homage at her feet,—
What, daring dreamer, what must you,
  When that bright face and form you meet,
Which, e'en Apelles would confess,
Surpass Campaspe's loveliness!

Then, Painter, fling thy tablet by,
And quickly from th' enchantress fly,
Ere 'round thy heart the spell is woven,
  That sterner spirits oft hath caught,
And, to their rashness, haply proven
  Her charms are with destruction fraught!
For though her face is fairer far
Than earthly flower or heavenly star,—
Yet, to thy bold, aspiring heart,
That holds in life a lowly part,
She is but one of those bright forms,—
A rainbow in a sky of storms!—
  That, from *afar*, the vision bless,
But never nearer come or smile,—
  That man may kneel to—not caress!—

A verdant, pure, but lonely isle,
  Encradled in a distant sea,
By which, perchance, some barque may gleam,
And catch its light, as in a dream,
  But with it cannot stay !
And though the voyager long may weep
For that bright Eden of the deep,
  And thirst its charms again to view,—
To hear once more its music sweet,—
  To rove its fragrant bowers anew,—
And watch the fond waves 'round it beat,
And all its treasures to obtain,—
Yet aye must find his longings vain !

"WHY WEEP FOR THE YOUNG?"

Why weep for the young and the lovely who die,
In the morning of life, ere the light from the sky,
The pure light of childhood, has flown, or a ray
Of innocence beaming, has vanished away,—
Ere the young, joyous heart, of unkindness hath heard,
Or hope falls exhausted, like a wing-broken bird :—
Ere sin and temptation, the sirocs of life,
Have blasted their beauty—or sorrow and strife,
O'er the morn-dreams of fancy their shadows have
flung,
Like pinions of evil ;—why weep for the young?

Why weep for the young—whose spirits, too pure,
The darkness of guilt and of grief to endure,
From the blightings of earth, from its changes and
crimes,
Have fled far away to the heavenly climes ;
Where youth, and affection, and all that is bright,
Drink from fountains of bliss ; and the pureness of
light

Sheds its beams of effulgence and beauty abroad,
O'er the brows of the sinless, like the smilings of
God :—
Where hosannas and blessings eternal are sung
From the flame-lips of cherubs,—why weep for the
young ?

Why weep for the young—who, like clouds of the
morn,
In incense and beauty to heaven are borne,—
And rise, 'mid the splendor and first blush of day,
From the darkness and travail of after decay,—
Nor gather and wait till the coming of even,
'Mid tempest and thunder and gloom to be riven,—
But pure and undarkened, in the orient gold,
Seek the source of all brightness, their hues to unfold,
Unscathed and unruffled by sorrow or wrong—
The dowers of earth ;—why weep for the young ?

Why weep for the young—the flowers of spring—
The birds that have ceased in the forest to sing—
But now in the bowers of Eden above,
Keep festivals ever of gladness and love :—

The stars of existence, whose beams on us here,
The far-climes of glory now still more endear :—
Oh ! surely 'tis sweet for affection to know,
That the lov'd and the bright are free from earth's wo,
And with seraphs and saints they swell the glad song·
Disconsolate mourner,—why weep for the young ?

THE FATED CITY.

'Twas evening,—and the gorgeous sun
  Streamed brightly in the sky,
And cast his farewell beams abroad,
Like smiles of an approving god,
  O'er plain, and mountain high,—
O'er waving fields of floating gold,
That round his sinking car were rolled,
And o'er the City's glistening spires,
That flashed beneath his blazing fires!

There lay that city,—wealth and pride
  Had built their temples there,
And swift-winged commerce there had brought,
From many a clime, her trophies caught,—
  From isles in ocean far,—
The tribute of the Indian seas,—
The offerings of the Cyclades,—
And jewels far outvying them,—
The mind's immortal diadem!

The sun went down, and night came o'er
  That city's winding walls ;
The white moon rose along the sky,
And looked down, like a spirit's eye,
  Upon the shouting halls,
Where beauty shone, and laughter went
From lip to lip, with music blent,—
Where all was heedless, happy, light,
Besporting on that festal night.

Within a palace, proud and high,
  A bridal band were met,—
Nowhere, beneath the blue-arched heaven,
Were happier hearts than then were given
  In union pure and sweet :
He was a warrior young but tried—
The City's peerless Rose,—the Bride !—
Long years of bliss and joy were theirs,
If aught availed fond friendship's prayers !

Throughout that city all was glad !—
  Wreaths for the young and gay,
Robes for the royal, —gems and stars,
To glitter o'er the warrior's scars, —

The poet's verdant bay !—
Ah, it is beauty's festal time !—
List, to the lover's melting rhyme !—
Fair city, ne'er, in all thy bliss,
Knew'st thou a happier night than this !

An hour passed on,—what cry is that,
Which thrills that city so ?—
What shrieks are those ?—what means yon cloud,
That veils the heavens, like a shroud,—
Blotting the moon's pure glow ?
What mean those flames, that blazing run
Along yon mountain dark and dun ?—
Why shakes the earth—why heaves the sea—
Why peal those thunders dreadfully ?

Night left the earth—the sun arose,
As wont, upon the sky,
And looked—not on that city bright,
Which he had left before the night,
With turrets gleaming high,—
But on a black and cheerless waste,
Dread desolation's hand had traced,—
Upon a flood of *lava*, where
Once stood, in splendor, POMPEII fair.

TO "THE ROSE OF CHARLESTON."

After a Ball.

Sweet Rose of Charleston! though the hours
  Were few and fleet in which we met,
Yet they were strewed with brilliant flowers,
  Whose hues and fragrance linger yet.
Amid the gay and circling dance,
  You passed with such bewitching grace,
That even now, in memory's glance,
  I view your fair Madonna face!

Sweet Rose of Charleston! other forms
  Were glittering 'round, a beauteous train,
As bright as rainbows after storms,
  When sunset smiles upon the rain;
But thou wert peerless in thy pride,
  The noblest, queenliest form of all;
In vain with thee the loveliest vied,—
  Young Aphrodite of the Ball!

Sweet Rose of Charleston! all the grace
  And lustre of these sunny skies,

Is pictured in thy smiling face,
  And beams resplendent in thine eyes.
The wild rose dimples on thy cheek,
  Blent with the lily's spotless hue ;
Thy lips like crimson blossoms speak ;
  Thine eyes are blue-bells bathed in dew !

Sweet Rose of Charleston ! in thine ear
  I breathed a few vain, idle words,
Such, as in sport, you often hear
  From Fancy's light, vibrating chords.
But in my heart I deeply felt
  The influence of a purer fire,
That made to love its pulses melt,
  As throbbed with music Memnon's Lyre !

Sweet Rose of Charleston ! never more
  In life, perchance, our paths may meet,
But on the sea, or on the shore,
  Thy beauty I shall ever greet :
Thy face is pictured on my brain,
  By memory's fond Daguerrean art ;
And, 'till my life shall cease, the chain
  Of love will ever bind my heart !

THE LIGHTNING-SLAIN.

Friend of my youth !—
Last eve, I stood beside thy grave,
Where verdant willows, drooping, wave,
In silent ruth ;—
And, as I gazed, I felt my eye-lids swell
With tears;—unwonted gushings from my bosom's well!

'Twas sunset's hour !—
Along the occidental sky,
Like ships at anchor, clouds did lie,—
While a thick shower
Of gold, o'er all their canvas, fell like fire,
And, like a town in flames, glowed the sun's funeral pyre !

Bright o'er the earth,
The radiance fell,—o'er sea and plain,
That blushed the glory back again !—
'Twas Vesper's birth !—
Entranced I gazed, my hand upon thy urn,
And felt lost thoughts of thee, within my bosom burn !

'Twas such an eve,
When last I looked upon thy brow,
So calm, and clear, and sunny in its glow!
To frown or grieve,
Thou ne'er hadst learnt,—thy free and boyish heart
Seemed, in its innocence, to be, of heaven, a part!

Thy, wild, gay laugh
Was like a minstrel's song,—thine eye
Dark as the midnight's moonless sky!
Thou loved'st to quaff
The bubbling cup of joy,—and science poured
Her fruits and treasures in thy mind,—a sumptuous hoard!

Before thine eye,
The world outspread, hued like the West,
That then, in gorgeous drapery drest,
Pillared the sky!—
And thou built castles grand, and fondly deemed
The flowering Palestine would prove all that it seemed!

We parted then,—
But storm and darkness ruled the night!—
The sun went down in kingly light.—
And mount and glen
Quaked, as the thunder rolled, and lightnings flashed,
And many a tall, old oak, by the dread bolts. was crashed!

Thy friends around,—
Thou, then, wast seated in thy home,
Smiling beneath thy parent dome,—
Love's hallowed ground;—
When, quick as thought, death's lightning arrow sped,
And hurled destruction, on thy fair and youthful head!

Next morn, I saw
Thy corpse!—Thy beauteous brow and cheek
Were pale and cold,—but pure and meek.
No stain or scar
Was on thy loveliness,—the vanished breath,
And pulseless heart were all that token'd death!

Thy SOUL was fled !
And sadly, to thy grave, we bore thee,—
O'er which, last eve, I did deplore thee !
Though thou art dead,
Long, long, will many an eye be dim, and long
Will memory wake her harp, for thee, in tears and song !

TO A YOUNG LADY.

How beautiful, fair girl, art thou,
All robed in innocence and truth!
Upon thy calm and snowy brow,
Beam, like a crown, the smiles of youth;
Heaven's sunshine falls and lights thy way,
As one too pure and bright for sorrow—
And virtue's soft and seraph ray
Flings lustre on thy dawning morrow—
Giving a promise, that thy life
Will ever be, with pleasure, rife!

Upon those dark, bright eyes of thine,
That, soft as moonlit waters, beam,
I love to gaze, and, as they shine,
Of those ethereal beings dream,
That oft, on us, have smiled, in sleep,
Then quickly flown, and made us weep,
That e'er to man, so much of heaven
Should just be shown,—ah! never given!

How soft the rose upon thy cheek,
  Blent with the lily's milder hue,
Whose mingling tints of beauty speak
  A sinless spirit—calm and true!—
The smile, that wreathes thy rosy lip,
  Is young affection's radiant token—
Beauty and Truth in fellowship!—
  The symbol of a heart unbroken;
Within thy bosom, holy thought,
  As in a temple, hath its shrine,
Refulgent with a glory caught
  From the pure presence of thy mind,
Whose lustre flings a hallowing ray,
Around thee, calm as orient day!

Oh! may thy life be ever bright,
  As aught thine early dreams have framed,
And not a shadow dim its light,
  Till heaven, in mercy, shall have claimed
Thee, as a being fit for naught
That earth can boast, all sorrow-fraught
As are its brightest visions. May
  Thy life be one long dream of love,

Unbroken till the perfect day,
  When heaven shall waft thy soul above,
And crown thee as an angel *there*,
Who wast indeed an angel *here!*

CARMEN SECULARÉ.

A Carrier's Address.

Another wave of Time has rolled
  Upon Eternity's wide ocean ;
Another funeral bell has tolled,
  With solemn sound and mighty motion ;
Another year is dead and gone,
  And with the Past lies coldly sleeping ;
But still another one comes on,
  With rainbow smiles, to cheer our weeping !
Then while we're mourning o'er *his* fate,
  Let rapture with our grief combine,—
And, as we sigh for Forty-Eight,
  We'll welcome Forty-Nine !

The year that's dead saw many things
  Pass o'er the earth in wild confusion ;
It saw the fall of mighty kings,—
  All Europe wrapt in Revolution :
Fair France sprang up in queenly pride,
  And trod in dust the Bourbon banner,—
And o'er the Seine's ensanguined tide,
  Was heard young freedom's loud hosanna !

Oh, Land of Lillies !—stand elate !
  The Warrior, and the Bard are thine !
And may their hopes in Forty-Eight,
  Prove true in Forty-Nine !

But o'er the sea the sky is dark,
  And gloomy clouds hang on the Island,
Where perished freedom's fragile bark,—
  Where Tara's harp is crushed and silent !
Woe ! for the scenes the year beheld,
  When prowled in gore the Saxon lion :—
And Mitchell's lordly heart, unquelled
  With Meagher sank, and proud O'Brien !
Oh land of woes !—disconsolate—
  A felon's heritage seems thine—
But what you lost in Forty-Eight,
  Redeem in Forty-Nine !

Our country, when the year was new,
  Was mingling in the strife of battle,—
But safe our victor-eagle flew
  Above the cannon's deadly rattle.
Peace was achieved,—and freedom's beams

Shone o'er new realms and territories,
And now the far Pacific streams
Reflect our country's bannered glories !
Yes, we have won a rich estate,—
Lo ! California's golden mine !—
Oh may the deeds of Forty-Eight
Be blessed in Forty-Nine !

But ah ! the year that now has gone,
Has had its grief as well as gladness,
And lips, that laughed with music's tone,
Awhile must breathe the dirge of sadness !
'Tis sad to see a chieftain's fall,—
'Tis sad to see a friend's defection,—
Sad is " Salt River" unto all—
Yes doubly sad a lost election !
Democracy has met this fate,—
The lordliest sun had its decline !—
But suns, that sank in Forty-Eight,
Will rise in Forty-Nine !

But life has other scenes than these,
Though humbler, dearer to the bosom,—

Where wave the heart's green vernal trees,
  And all the young affections blossom !
The year just passed has held the torch
  Of Love full oft in Hymen's bowers,
And oh ! perhaps, through death's dark porch,
  Some friends have gone—no longer ours !
Smiles blend with tears !—the woof of fate !—
  The yew and myrtle oft entwine !
But may the tears of Forty-Eight
  Prove smiles in Forty-Nine !

Thanks to the breezes of the sky,
  They've fanned with health our orange bowers,
And o'er our land Prosperity
  Has thrown her robes of grain and flowers !
What though the Plague's dark angel now,
  Upon a sister city's treading,
And scattering ashes on her brow,
  And sackcloth o'er her beauty spreading,—
We, while we mourn her dreadful fate,
  May humbly kneel before the shrine,
And trust our God in Forty-Eight
  Will shield in Forty-Nine !

Our "little city's" steeples now
  Flash joyous in the New Year's splendor,—
The crown of Commerce decks her brow,
  And hopes of "better days" attend her.
The high designs of Art and Trade
  Have wooed the Ocean Steamships nigh her,
And soon bold effort will have made
  The Railroad to the far Ohio!
The Fair Emporium of our State
  In pride and opulence will shine,
When these, the *dreams* of Forty-Eight,
  Are *facts* in Forty-Nine!

But, friends, I linger in my song
  Much longer than I fear is civil,
For poetry's a bore, when long,
  Though sung and written by the "*Devil.*"
But yet, before I make my bow,
  One gentle HINT I must not smother,—
I've sang for you these verses now,
  And "one good turn deserves another."
Thanks!—double thanks!—May kindest fate
  Make every earthly blessing thine,
And twice the joy of Forty-Eight
  Be yours in Forty-Nine!

BIRD OF THE SOUTH.

An Allegory: for Mrs. Caroline Lee Hentz.

Bird of the South!—though thy beautiful pinions
  Have flashed on mine eyes, like the wings of a star,—
And ne'er have I seen, save in fancy's dominions,
  A phantom of light so exquisitely fair:

Though soft is thine eye as the blue of thy heaven,
  Thy motions in grace like the stoop of the breeze,—
Though round thee a halo of beauty is woven,
  That brightens, like moonshine, thy home in the trees!

Yet, Bird of the South,—strange and beautiful vision!—
  'Tis not for these charms that I follow thy flight,—
There still is about thee a spell more Elysian
  Than all that have flashed on my wondering sight!

Last eve, as I mused by the door of my dwelling,— eeəə
  While stars, through the forest, like spirit lamps, beamed,
I heard in the distance a music excelling
  All melody ever rapt fancy had dreamed!

It rose on the air like the hymn of an angel,—
  It fell on my heart like a silvery rain ;—
It banished the griefs that encumbered my manhood,
  And brought back the bowers of Eden again !

Oh, wild as the dream of the wandering prophet,
  The raptures that song to my breast did impart ;
I saw the bright ladder descending from heaven,
  And felt the good angels come down in my heart.

That song was thine own one, sweet bird of the distance !
  Fair Bird of the South ! that wild minstrelsy thine
Thine, thine is the art that can sweeten existence,
  With spells of the angeis,—with music divine !

Then, Bird of my-own-land ! pour forth thy wild numbers,
  And gladden the sky with its sabbath again !
Though bright are thy pinions— the music that slumbers
  In the breast of the minstrel, more homage will gain !

MY MOTHER'S GRAVE.

The fount from which my being flowed,—
  The calm, pure fount of life and love,—
The star that o'er my cradle glowed,
  And beamed my boyhood's path above,—
Have ceased from earth—and lonely now—
Oh, mother !—o'er thy grave I bow !

From childhood's dawn, to manhood's hour,
  Thy tender love was still my guide,—
It nurtured first the opening flower,
  And all my infant wants supplied,—
Yes, every life-pulse of my heart
Drew from thy breast its vital part !

What visions of my infant years,
  What scenes of love, what sounds of joy,
What prayers, caresses, smiles, and tears,—
  What counsels to the wayward boy !—
Now swim before my care-worn eyes,
While bending where my mother lies !

Her high, pale brow, her patient smile,
  Her lips, where tenderest kisses hung,
Her graceful form, though bent awhile,
  So queenly when her life was young—
All pass athwart my throbbing brain,
And bring her image back again!

I see her by my father's side,
  In holiest love and union blest;
I see them smiling in their pride,
  O'er happy children 'round them pressed,—
And now, with fond parental care,
They kneel in morn and evening prayer!

Oh, she was all that's brightest—best—
  So "pure in heart," so rich in mind,—
Of every social worth possessed,
  By every Christian grace refined—
Faultless she filled her part below
And passed where only such may go!

She's passed to heaven—but oh how dark
  The sky from which her smile has gone—

No star now lives to guide my bark,
  No fount to cheer my spirit on !—
Yet, 'till my life shall cease to be,
Her memory shall abide with me !

1853.

LE BON TEMPS VIENDRA!

A Motto on a Ring.

Though sad our hearts at parting now,
  As well such loving hearts may be!
Though sorrow shadows either brow,
  And time spreads forward gloomily:
Though months may pass without delight,
  Like nights without a single star,
Yet, still, my love, let hope be bright,
  For oh, *le bon temps viendra!*

The happy days I've passed with thee,
  Like Sabbaths bright, have o'er me flown!
These scenes have Edens seemed to me,
  And thou, my Eve, my joy, my own!
Yet oh, a deeper gloom they'd fling,
  Like Paradise beheld afar,
If heard I not an angel sing,—
  Hope on! *Le bon temps viendra!*

Yes, dearest, though for months we part,
  The future holds one gladdening light,

Whose rays shall bless my lonely heart
'Mid separation's gloomy night.
Its beams through time and distance reach,—
Bright prophets on a golden car !—
And seem to breathe in gentlest speech,
Ah yes, *le bon temps viendra* !

Then smile away these gloomy fears,
These griefs that cloud that pearly brow ;
Let not those eyes be dimmed with tears,
Nor sadness shade thy beauty now !
In faith and hope, the time abide,—
The advent of the joyous star,—
For oh, across the future's tide,
Sweet love, *le bon temps viendra !*

Oh yes, the time of joy *shall* come,
With sweeter scenes and brighter skies !
The lamps of love our hearts illume,
Reflected in thy smiling eyes !
Our souls united then shall own
An ecstacy no grief can mar,—
And feel how sweet the gentle tone,
That sang *le bon temps viendra !*

THE NATAL STAR.

Its was a faith believed of old,
   That when a spirit left the sky,
In human beauty to unfold,
   A star assumed a place on high :
That o'er the angel, thus earth-given,
   That star with guardian brightness shone,
Swaying its destinies, 'till heaven
   Reclaimed the wanderer as its own !

Thus, lady, o'er thy cradle beamed
   A star, with mild, auspicious ray,
Whose beauty has but brighter gleamed
   With each returning natal day :
Now, all unclouded, from its throne,
   It greets again, at this sweet hour,
The cherub to a woman grown,—
   The bud unfolded to a flower !

That star has seen thy girlish grace
   Developing itself in love ;

Its beams have lit thy maiden face,
  With light and beauty from above.
Sweet pleiad, with prophetic glow,
  It now illumes the Future's sky,
And, like a sibyl, smiles to show
  How blest thy life will wander by!

Oh! may that star, with gentlest ray,
  Thus ever keep its sweet control;
No cloud to dim its diamond ray,—
  Its beauty mirrored in thy soul!
And oft, as each revolving year
  Shall bring thy joyous birthday round,
Still smile as sweet on thy career,—
  Still find thy brow with roses crowned!

TO EGERIA.

An Unknown Correspondent.

Sweet Spirit ! though, upon my vision,
  Thy starry eyes have never beamed,
And only, in some hour Elysian,
  My heart has of thy beauty dreamed :
Though, like the nymph of Roman fable,
  Thy words alone have reached mine ear,—
Sweet as the songs that sinless Abel
  In Eden's twilight paused to hear,—
Yet still my soul thine influence feels,
And, Numa-like, before thee kneels !

Oh, Spirit Love ! thy viewless pinions
  Are rustling 'round my forehead now,—
I hear thy song in Love's dominions,
  And feel thy breath upon my brow !—
My soul is tranced !—the love is strongest
  That weaves its spell around the *soul !*—
Celestial !—'twill endure the longest,—
  Exempt from earth and time's control !—

Then let me gaze upon thine eyes,
And on thy brow's young Paradise!

Fondly, last night, in troubled slumbers,
My spirit sought the destined spot,—
There sweetly, still, in magic numbers,
I heard thy song, but found *thee* not,
Oh, nymph and angel! why deceive me?—
Why not the promised trysting keep?—
Why, of thy beauty thus bereave me,—
Even in "the pictured land of sleep?"
I yearn,—I die,—thy form to press,
Unearthly in its loveliness!

The "emerald waves," in dimples gleaming,
Still lave, like love, that beauteous shore,—
The angeled stars, from bright urns beaming,—
Their liquid silver on it pour!—
Love calls again!—oh, viewless spirit,—
Such deep devotedness requite,—
Let me the bliss of heaven inherit,
Clasping thy beauty *there* to-night.
My heart will own no love beside,
But kneel to thee, my Spirit Bride!

ELEGY,

On a Mocking-Bird killed by a Cat.

Weep for the feathered minstrel gone
 The woodland wit, the poet wild,
The troubadour of silver tone,
 Euterpé's winged and frolic child !—
His song is hushed, his gay laugh done,
 His bright eye motionless and dim ;
No more his fair wings glint the sun ;
 The Loved of beauty,—weep for him !

From honeysuckle groves he came,
 From wooing eyes, to gaze on hers ;
To syllable in song her name,
 And shame her duller worshippers :
And not in vain his ardent love,—
 He won the lady's homage deep ;
She prized her *bird* all *beaux* above ;
 But he is dead,—then for him weep !

Ah yes ! how oft in shade and sun,
 I've seen her with the winged bard play,

Forgetful of the human one,
  Who envious gazed his soul away !
And oh ! what tones that bird would breathe,
  When playing with her cherry lips !—
As who would not !—yet mourn his death,
  For 'twas a sudden, sad eclipse !

One mild and rosy summer eve,
  When revelling in light and song,
With but one tone that seemed to grieve
  His beauteous mistress absent long,—
As through the room his voice he flung,
  In tones would craze a Malibran,
The parlor-tiger on him sprung,
  And WILLIE was "a ruined man !"

Yet bright his life ! her smiles by day
  Were more than flowers or song to him,
And, through the night, his amorous lay,
  Around her dreaming couch, would swim:
And oh ! what glimpses met his eye,
  Of charms but dreamed by other swains !—
If I such beauty could espy,
  Grimalkin too might end my pains !

Yet mourn for him !—Ye rival bards,
  In gushing strains of sorrow weep !
His fate,—alas ! like Chatetard's,—
  Ye should in long remembrance keep :
For had he never shaped his breath
  To amorous odes, 'round Beauty's shrine,
He had not met his cruel death,
  Nor filled this *cat-a-logue* of mine !

Then Willie mourn ! for she will weep
  Her poet-pet, whose songs are o'er ;
Oh ! sweet as Ovid's be his sleep,
  Where cats and beaux shall vex no more !
I mourn him too,—yet own my tears
  Are like my numbers, *somewhat flat*,—
For through the shades, my fancy hears
  The Mock-bird crying—'*Scat! escat!*

A VALENTINE.

May I, as thy Valentine,
Lady fair,—
Place upon thy pictured shrine,
Votive song and flower of mine,
Which may have, through grace of thine,
Welcome there ?

Months have passed since last we met,
Lady fair :
But my heart cannot forget ;
On its page thy seal is set,
And it views thy beauty yet,
Everywhere !

All thy gentleness and grace,
Lady fair ;
Fairy form and angel face,—
Such as dreaming painters trace,—
In my memory keep a place,—
Pictured there !

Not an evening passes by,
Lady fair,
But I turn my weary eye,
Sadly to yon Western sky,
And, in lonely yearning, sigh
"She is there!"

Thou art to me as a star,
Lady fair;
Which I kneel to from afar;
May no cloud thy beauty mar;
And, upon thy golden car,
Hear my prayer!

May thy life be ever bright,
Lady fair,
Clasped in Love's resplendent light,
Never doomed to sorrow's night,—
Disappointment's withering blight,—
Grief or care!

TO A DARK-EYED GEORGIAN.

My-dark eyed Georgian !—I have gazed
On beauty's wildest forms,
Who lit life's pathway with their rays,
As rainbows circle storms—
Entranced, have knelt in Persian faith,
Before their starry light,
And hailed them with my spirit's breath—
The beautiful—the bright !
Oh, woman's form was ever dear
Unto this trembling heart :
She seemed an angel sent to cheer
Man's else unfriended part—
But ne'er till I beheld thy face—
Sweet peri of my path—
Did I imagine what sweet grace
Celestial woman hath !

Yes, dark-eyed Georgian—when mine eyes
In pleasure's festal hour,
First saw thine image sweetly rise,

With all its queenly dower
Of charms, might win an anchorite
To leave his thoughts of heaven,
And be content with earthly light—
To smile, though unforgiven !—
I felt that all my heart had framed,
When rapt in dreams elysian,
Was far surpassed in loveliness,
By thee—ecstatic vision !
No more were other faces fair,
No more my heart was free—
All I had ever yearned to share
Was centred sweet in thee.

But, dark-eyed Georgian—not alone,
Is beauty's impress thine—
Thy face is mind's imperial throne,
Thy heart is Virtue's shrine.
The gift of goodness and of love,
Of holy hopes and thought,
Belongs to thee—not heaven above
Has hearts more richly fraught !
Thy own beloved and sunny clime—
Clime of fair and free !—

Hath breathed its influence in thy heart—
  Is shadowed forth in thee !
Its chiming waters tune thy voice,
  Its roses tint thy lip,
Its sweetest scenes and sounds are thine,
  In chastened fellowship !

Then, dark-eyed Georgian,—deign to smile
  Upon thine humble bard,
Whose heart and harp, entranced the while,
  Will find a sweet reward ;
And should thy beauty never be
  Unto his longing given,
Fondly he will remember thee,
  As saints a dream of heaven !
And oft, within his backwoods' home,
  Beneath the Western Star,
At eve thy memory shall come,
  And bless him from afar !
And then his lyre shall proudly wake
  Its votive numbers wild,
And hail thee still, with homage deep,
  As Georgia's loveliest child !

TO ANGELINA, WITH A BIBLE.

A Versified Incident.

My innocent and lovely child,
  At parting, claimed a gift from me,
And as her blue eyes sweetly smiled,
  I asked her " Love, what shall it be ?"
She quick replied, in accents mild,
  " An *Arbor Vitæ* sprig from thee."

What ! only that ? No sparkling gem ?
  No toy, nor wreath, nor jewelry ?
No treasure which, when shewn to them,
  Thy playmates shall with envy see ?"
Her sweet reply was still the same,
  " An *Arbor Vitæ* sprig from thee."

" Well, dearest, 'tis a strange request,
  From one so artless, young, and free ;
The only mandate of thy breast,

An emblem of my love for thee :
Yet I will grant the fond behest,—
"An *Arbor Vitæ* sprig from me!"

So here it is, but with it take
Another from a kindred tree—
"*The Tree of Life,*"—whose leaves will make
More fadeless bowers of love for thee :
Oh, keep it for thy father's sake,
This *Arbor Vitæ* gift from me!

TO VIRGINIA.

Beauty ! other lips are breathing
   Vows of gentlest love to thee ;
Other eyes bright smiles are wreathing,
   Which thine own responsive see ;
Brows, still fair with boyhood's beauty,
   Vail them at thy flowery feet,—
"Love for thee, their pride, their duty !"—
   Such the song their lips repeat.

How can I, then, lone and saddened,—
   Gone the spring-time of my heart,—
Hope to see thy young brow gladdened
   By the praise I could impart ?
No, my words would sink in silence,
   'Mid the music 'round thee poured ;
Or, like birds o'er blossomed islands,
   Pass unheeded and unheard !

Yet, believe me, young and dimpled
  Beauty, with the laughing eyes,—
Willowed springs, clear and unrimpled,
  Holding spots of sunny skies,—
That no heart before thee bending,
  Proffering prayer, and song, and sigh,—
Vow and praise in worship blending,—
  Loves thee half so well as I!

FLORENCE.

I.

Behold where sky and water meet,
A star is twinkling low and sweet !—
Its rays have shone, for one brief hour,
Unequalled in its azure bower !—
Lo ! now it sinks in beauty lone,—
Smiles a minute and is gone !
From us is gone,—but oh, 'tis given
A morning light to another heaven !

II.

How like to it, the angel child,
Who, for a minute, with us smiled !—
Upon the verge of life just beamed,—
A heavenly emanation seemed !—
Then faded from our gazing eyes,
Leaving lone and dark our skies !
Yet oh, sweet thought—she too is given
A morning light to another heaven !

LOVE'S EMBLEMS.

A star upon the brow of heaven,
  In peerless beauty glowing ;
A rose round which the breeze of even,
  With sighs of love, is flowing ;
A harp whose melting music sweet
  Is won by trembling fingers ;
A verdant blest and pure retreat,
  Where virgin nature lingers ;
Are, lady, emblems true of thee,—
Of fragrance, music, light and purity !

A cloud by fitful breezes driven,
  Athwart a dark and wintry sky ;
A tree by lightning rudely riven,
  And left in loneliness to die ;
A bird, that falls with pinion broken,
  Far from the nest that gave him birth ;
Love's once remembered, treasured token,
  Now left to moulder on the earth ;
Are emblems of the bard, whose hand
Now strikes his broken lyre at thy command !

The star will burn forever bright;
The cloud through storm, must wander;
The rose will smile 'mid Spring's delight;
The tree fall 'neath the thunder;
Long will the harp with music gush;
The bird ne'er lift his pinion;
Sweet nature's scene with brightness blush;
Revive not love's dominion;
Such is the difference, lady fair,
Between the lots that thou and I must share!

Yet, sometimes, lady, when those viewest
A cloud float by a silver star;
Or hear'st a lone bird, in the forest,
Sigh to a rose his music prayer:
Or see'st amid some lovely scene,
A blasted tree stand sad and lonely;
Remember him, whose heart, once sheen,
Is sorrow's now, and sorrow's only,—
And who, although he asks not fame,
Would have thee sometimes gently breathe his name.

TO A BEAUTIFUL STRANGER.

From "The Croakers in Washington."

As, sailing over Southern seas,
  The pilgrim views some beauteous island,
Verdant with groves of fragrant trees
  And grassy slope and sunny highland,
That smiles beneath the tropic-heaven,
  An Eden, yet to man ungiven ;
As, in some blue and balmy night,
  When all the sky with stars is golden,
The gazer sees some orb more bright
  Float newly out amid the olden ;
Or as, in some old prophet's dream,
  An angel stooped before his vision,
With eyes as blue as Hebron's stream,
  And form and features all elysian :
So, lovely stranger, on mine eyes,
  And in mine heart, hath shone thy beauty,
With all this sudden, sweet surprise,—
With all this birthright of the skies,—
  Till Love for thee hath grown a duty !

And yet, fair one, I know thee not,—
  As strangers we have met and parted ;
My shadow ne'er has dimmed thy thought,
Thine ear the words hath never caught,
  Of praise, that on my lips have started,
Though oft in brilliant halls I've seen
  Thy form amid the gay and witty,
Yet I am sure that brow serene
  Knew not that I was—" in the city !"
Yes, in the " White House," 'mid the press
  Of belles and fops and politicians,
I've watched thy form, all gracefulness,
  Glide to the spell of the musicians.
One night—perhaps you may recall
  The scene—last winter at *Carusi's*,—
I stood like Lara by the wall,
  You like Calypso 'mid the Muses ;
Though all the forms around were bright,
  And bright the candles and peonies,
I knew not whence arose the light,
  Or if the music were *Korponay's* ;
I only saw those sapphire eyes,
  Amid thy blushes, sweetly burning,

And envied all,—their destinies,
  On whom thy gentle smiles were turning.
Again I saw that beauteous brow,—
Than the Madonna's softer now,
  Bend lily-like within the temple ;
And, while your thoughts own'd heaven s control,
Mine, truant, heard not Mr. Spr——le,
  But dreamed about thy rosy dimple !

One eve too, when the sunset's shade
  Around the Capitol was playing,
I met thee on the Esplanade,
  And saw thee 'neath the Elm trees straying :
Though green the sward, and cool the trees,—
  Thanks to the art of *Jemmy Maher !*
Yet none of them my heart could please
  When thou wert absent, lovely strayer !
But all in vain !—you little guess
  The thoughts thus dwelling in my bosom,—
Like flowers that in some wilderness,
  For distant stars, unheeded blossom !
For though I've heard thy sweet *name* spoken
From gentle lips, it is to me a stranger's token !

Yes we are strangers ; far apart
  Our paths through life have been divided,
As streams that from far fountains start,
  And only once have nearer glided.
My home is far, where orange bowers,
  In green and golden beauty, bloom ;
When birds and blossoms fill the hours
  With song, and lustre, and perfume :
By Mexic's soft and sunny sea,
  Whose waters lapse on silver sand,
And skies, as bright as skies may be,
  Curve sweetly o'er an Eden land.
Thy childhood's smiling scene reposes
Beneath the sunset's glowing roses,—
Where limpid rivers glide along,
Through hills of green, in light and song,
And prairie flowers their sweets exhale,
Like richest incense, on the gale.—
Their loveliness those skies have given,
As almoners of bounteous heaven,
To frame thy form, thy mind, thy heart,
With all the wealth they could impart.
There is thy home, thy hopes, thy love,—
  Oh treasury of sweet affections !

And there thy gentlest fancies rove,
  To cull the heart's best recollections.
But, beauteous maiden, could I gain
  Thy smiles, to light my Southern dwelling,
I then should, Paris-like, obtain
  A treasure all its wealth excelling.
But no ! such dreams 'tis vain to tell ;—
We are but strangers,—fare-the-well !

WASHINGTON CITY, 1845.

THE CAPITOL BY MOONLIGHT.

From "The Croakers in Washington,"

"If thou wouldst view fair Melrose aright,
Go visit it by the pale moonlight."—*Scott.*

How beautiful the sky to-night!
The moon is forth in all her glory;
And, white as snow, her waves of light
Roll sweetly 'round yon terraced height,
As when of old, in Grecian story,
She stooped upon the hills of Thrace,
To kiss Endymion's sleeping face:
Then come, sweet one, and let us stray
Beside yon lofty walls, to-night,
That in the moonlight lift away,
With column, arch, and architrave,
With pillared dome, and sculptured nave,
More beautiful and grand than those
The Wizard saw by "fair Melrose,"
When half in shadow, half in beam,
They gave his timbrel's sweetest theme;

Or Albion's Pilgrim sadly viewed,
When by the Cæsar's halls he stood,
And heard from far the monks' *te deum*
Float, dirge-like, through the Coliseum !

You smile, sweet one, that thus my heart
  Grows sentimental as we wander ;—
Well, at your jest, such thoughts depart,
  And different topics we will ponder.
We're on the terrace ; gaze below,—
  How silent sleeps the Federal City !
With all its crowds of great and low,
  Its belles and fops, its weak and witty !
From far Potomac's silvery stream,
Just glimmering in yon random beam,—
To here where Tiber creeps along,
Immortal made in *Little's* song,
As "Goose-creek once,"—your eye may see
The far-famed city of the Free !
Wide is the view,—but at our feet
Its loveliest scenes in softness meet.
These verdant groves, these grassy lawns,
  These founts that in the moonlight play,

These trellised bowers which art adorns,—
These walks that wind through flowers away—
All form a scene, which might be famed,
Like Valambrosa's myrtle glades,—
Or else an Eden fitly named,
With all its moonlit banks and shades,—
But here,—in Democratic sounds,—
Is only styled the "Public Grounds!"

But why, sweet one, should thus my lip
Sport with the bathos of the scene,
When blest with thy companionship,
Thy radiant form and graceful mien?
Oh, turn thy face toward the heaven,
And let the moon sink in thine eyes,—
Fair founts,—to whose still depths are given
The loveliest secrets of the skies!
Yes, though bright forms around me
Are wandering on the esplanade,
And frequent falls the lover's vow,
In low, deep tones of homage paid,—
Though through yon trees their white robes glance,
Like angels in a prophet's trance,—

Yet none can equal thy fair form,
  Thy crescent brow and silken tresses !
Thine eyes with love-light sweetly warm,
  Those lips, this wanton breeze caresses !
No, not the bright shapes on these walls,—
  The Painter's and the Sculptor's Dreams,—
That decorate these stately halls,
  With Art's most weird and magic beams,—
  In Persico's or Weir's sweet themes,—
Can so my wandering heart impress,—
  (Columbus like by tempests hurled,)—
As thou, with thy pure loveliness,—
  The timid EVE of my New World !—
Can *thy* deep spells of love impart,—
ROSE STANDISH of my pilgrim heart !

But not for me such thoughts as these !
The boy may love the Pleiades,—
That nightly swarm of golden bees ;—
The brook may love the soaring moon,
  And shrine her in its trembling heart ;
The floweret love the wild-bird's tune,
  Brought by the breeze, but—to depart ;

The minstrel may uplift his wishes,
To gain the better "loaves and fishes,"
Reserved for politician's dishes ;
But I can never dream of thee,
But as the sea-shell of the sea,
Which, when afar 'tis rudely borne,
Will for its absent mistress mourn,
And in its wreathed heart retain
The echoes of her long-gone strain :
Or as some hungry Clerk recalls
The hours he spent in Treasury halls,
Ere the remorseless *guillotine*
His head and pocket passed between !

Well, be it so : if beauty's smile,
  The moonlight to a gloomy day,
May not my lonely heart beguile,
  There is for hope another way,
  "Ambition" shall assume the sway !
Then, "look out," lady !—in the years
  That journey up the hill of time,
The sun of Fame his crest uprears,
  And floods with light a halcyon clime !

Mayhap the bard, who by thee now
His nonsense and his music breathes,
Shall yet, around his pallid brow,
Entwine the oak and myrtle wreaths !
Things quite as strange have happ'd, they say ;
Yon lordly dome invites him on—
Where Benton, Webster, Polk, and Clay,
Calhoun, and Adams, have borne sway,
With many others of renown,—
And some have won the laurel crown.
Well, should it come, he'll meekly bear
The laurels he is doomed to wear,
And even then with joy recall
This eve beside the Capitol,
When, brighter than the queen of night,
Shone on his heart thy beauty's light,
And memory's moonlight then shall bless
His solitude's dark wilderness.

WASHINGTON, 1845.

ALBUM LEAVES.

I.

What is an Album ?—'Tis a shrine
Where Love may breathe his vows divine ;
Where Friendship may her garland place,
And Painting lines of magic trace ;
Where music may combine with Song,
The praise of Beauty to prolong ;
Where lips that smile, or brows that grieve,
Alike may their mementoes leave ;
And Bards, like me, unknown to fame,
May carve an else-forgotten name !

I like it well,—young Beauty's Book.
It is a glass, where many look ;—
First comes a brow beloved and fair,—
A mother's, sister's, brother's there !—
And now a face more brightly beams,
The image of her morning dreams !—

Now troops of friends pass smiling by,
With laughing cheek and kindling eye;
Till last, the shifting mirror shows
A Bard, *with spectacles on nose!*

Yes 'tis a glass! but oh it keeps
Each image that across it sweeps,
As in the magic of Daguerre,
The vision is imprinted there!
How priceless then!—As Memory's friend,
It will its kind assistance lend,
And serve, in after years, to show,
The friends beloved, "long, long ago!"
How blest, sweet one, I then shall be,
If you can "catch a glimpse" of me!

II.

Amid the flowers that deck this shrine,
  The gifts of Love and Friendship dear,
My heart, a simple *wreath* would twine,
  And fondly place the tribute here:

Each word should be a blossom sweet,
  Culled from the garden of the heart,
And ever, from this pure retreat,
  Perpetual incense should impart!

To none more lovely, could I give
  The votive wild flowers of my song,
For, in thy smiles only they live,
  As violets in the sunshine throng:
Thy brow is morning to their love,
  Thine eyes, the blue sky of the Spring,
Thy breath, the breeze that from above
  Brings health and sweetness on its wing.

The flowers of song!—by Love perfumed!
  How sweetly 'neath thine eyes they smile,
As Grecian blossoms brightest bloomed
  In Flora's own love-haunted isle!—
Mine are the humblest offered here,
  Yet in the wreath my hand has wrought,
Is one that breathes affection's prayer,
  The timid fond—*forget me not.*

III.

As, on some favorite forest tree,
  The wandering school-boy carves his name,
More pleased the record there to see,
  Than were it on the scroll of fame ;
So, lady, on this pictured shrine,
  The treasured Tablet of thy heart,—
With more delight I place my line,
  Than on the trophied page of art.

How sweet to think, in after time
  Thine eyes, so beautiful and bright,
Will smile upon my artless rhyme,
  And gild its letters with their light !
How pleasant too to know that then
  Thy rosy lips—should others blame—
Will prize this tribute of my pen,
  And kindly breathe the writer's name.

Could I but weave the threads of life
  To golden tissues, for thy sake—
All free from sorrow care or strife,
  A joyous destiny I'd make.

Thy fate should like this volume be,—
  Composed of pictures, songs, and flowers—
While friends should ever circle thee,
  And Love and pleasure wing thine hours !

IV.

As sings a bird in Beauty's bower,
  At evening's glad and golden time,
Pleased to delight for one short hour,
  Her spirit, by his artless rhyme :
So I would here, with kindred feeling,
  Amid these flowery leaves, impart
One strain of minstrelsy, revealing
  The gentlest wishes of my heart !

Oh, may the lady of this bower
  Be ever fair as she is now ;
May no unkind or evil Power
  E'er dim the beauty of her brow ;
May Hope and Love distribute roses
  Around her steps, where'er they move,
And angel pinions, when life closes,
  Convey her to the bowers above !

V.

What should a brother's offering be
  Upon a sister's shrine?
Not incense sweet of Araby,
  Nor gems from India's mine.
The incense on the gale is shed,
  And melts in sighs away;
The gem may sparkle on the head,
  But lends the heart no ray;
These then would ill befit a love
As pure as angels feel above!

What offering then should here be brought,
  Linked with a brother's name?
Some flower from fair Circassia caught?
  Some picture known to fame?
Oh, no, the flower would blush awhile,
  Then fade, and fall away;
The picture might awake a smile,
  But ne'er could grief allay;
Some other token sure should shine
Upon these sibyl leaves of thine!

The only offering I can bring,
  My sister, then, to thee,
Is one I would not give a king,
  Nor could he rend from me.
'Tis humble, poor, and little worth,
  To weave with songs and flowers,
But ah ! 'tis thine by love and birth,
  In joy's or sorrow's hours.
Then take, and with it never part,
For, JULIA, 'tis thy brother's heart !

VI.

As erst the cold Egyptian stone,
  At morning's smile awoke to life,
And breathed a soft melodious tone,
  With feeling and affection rife ;
So this unpolished verse of mine,
  Beneath thine eyes so bright and dear,
May gush with music in each line,
  And prove a fitting tribute here !

But not alone did Memnon's lyre,
  With beauty's praises gush and glow,

It thrilled with a prophetic fire,
  That promised peace and pleasure too :
Thus would my verse foretell for thee
  A bright and joyous path through life,
Fair woman's happiest destiny—
  Thrice blest, as daughter, sister, wife !

VII.

A forest bird, one moonlight night,
  Perched on a tree, by beauty's door,
And swinging there in wild delight,
  His sylvan numbers warbled o'er.
He seemed to strive her ear to please
By all his gentlest melodies,
And to enchant the listening maid,
With his untutored serenade !

Had I the music of that bird,
  Fair girl, for whom this song I wreathe,
How gladly in each glowing word,
  Would I thy praise and beauty breathe !
Thy gentleness and maiden grace,
Thy glowing charms of form and face,

In blended lustre here should meet,
And make e'en my rude numbers sweet.

But as it is, alas how vain
  My effort to delight thine ear!
How weak and worthless is the strain
  That I so idly scribble here :—
Less welcome than the wild-bird's tune,
My song will perish quite as soon,
And, with the morrow, in thy thought,
Both bard and bird will be forgot.

IRELAND.

A Fragment.—1848.

While thus our country, in her eagle flight,
Bears proudly upward to the Orb of Light,
Shall we, her sons, forget the claims of those,
Who now are struggling with oppression's woes?
No, o'er the waters of the Atlantic deep,
Our warmest sympathies, like ark-doves, sweep,
And, to the sufferers of the Emerald Isle,
Would bear the branch of love, and freedom's smile!
The land of Grattan, Curran, Emmet, Tone,—
The trampled footstool of a foreign throne!
Oh, blood of martyrs!—staining all her green,
Soon may ye wash her spotted garments clean!
The harp of Tara!—soon may it pour forth
The olden anthems through the island-north!—
And Emmet's epitaph ring o'er the sea—
"Erin Mavourneen!—thou art free—art free!"

THREE SONNETS.

I

EDITH.

Sweet SAXON maiden! in thy glowing face,
  Thy sky-lit eyes, and yellow locks that gleam
  In their rich folds, like some sunlighted stream,
The old ancestral heritage I trace!
No Southern blood has dimmed thy Northern grace!
  The island mother's beauty still is seen
  In thy white brow, and proud, yet modest, mien!
Bright emanation of the olden race!
That race has many trophies: its brave men
  Have, immemorial, been stern freedom's sons:
Their might has kept the tyrant in his den:—
  Race of the Sydneys and the Washingtons!
Their daughters, too, the fairest man may see!
And oh, sweet boast! their loveliest one in THEE!

II.

MARY.

Oh, for one dream of thee, mine early love !
  Come, in thy beauty, to my couch, to-night.
Lonesome and weary, like some prisoned dove,
  I pine, dejected, for thine eyes' sweet light !
  Oh, come, and make my darkened visions bright;
Wander in dream-land with my soul awhile ;
Pour on my heart the star-shine of thy smile,
  And wake its pulses into young delight !
What raptures once were ours ! what scenes of bliss !
  How fondly then our forms together clung,
How sweet the rose-breath of thy plighted kiss !
  What words of music on thy timid tongue !
Though they are gone, sleep may restore their light,
  Then come, in beauty, to my couch to-night !

III.

CAROLINE.

Sweet Caroline ! if, as the poet sings—
  A thing of beauty is a joy forever,
  And its pure loveliness decreaseth never ;

What wealth for memory thy beauty brings—
Brightest and loveliest of created things!
Yes! though my years now nearly double thine,
Thy life a rising star—fast sinking mine,
Yet, 'round my heart, thy childish beauty clings,
As some sweet dream that ne'er can pass away!
Those braided curls of gold, that eye's blue ray,
Brow, cheek, and lips serene will ever shine,
The sweetest gems and flowers on memory's shrine.
Then thanks to heaven, young visitant-elysian,
That thy rich beauty thus hath blest my vision!

A PORTRAIT.

Hand me my harp !—I'll wake once more
  Its silent chords for lady fair,
And strive the visions to restore,
  Which once came bright and freely there !

Be glad the strains !—for she who claims
  The minstrel's art, should know but joy ;
Her heart is filled with kindliest aims,
  And kindliest deeds her life employ.

In girlhood's smiling Eden yet,
  She lingers with the birds and flowers :
Her heart has never known Regret,—
  Oh, bright and sinless girlhood's hours !

Beneath her steps bright roses spring,—
  No cloud has dimmed her morning sky ;

The birds of hope, with gayest wing,
  Are ever flashing on her eye !

'Tis said that there are those in life,
  Who *make* the joy they cannot find,—
Amid a world of woe and strife,
  For this, was framed her gentle mind.

Sweet words are always on her lips,—
  The jewelry and flowers of thought !—
No orient pearls can these eclipse,—
  For these with mind and soul are fraught !

Her beauty's charms I cannot tell ;
  Although I feel them on my heart ;
They need, than mine, a loftier spell,—
  The painter's not the poet's art !

And yet, in all her loveliness,—
  Her outward charms, her inward light,—
I know not one so formed to bless,—
  To make life beautiful and bright.

Oh, may the gentle stars that guide
  The destinies of man, o'er her,
With kindliest influence, preside,—
  On her their choicest rays confer!

For oh, if these to her repay
  One half the joy she sheds around,
Sweet hopes will ever gild her way,
  And keep her heart with roses crowned!

LOVE'S LESSON.

There were two stars in heaven;
  They loved each other so,
That, as 'tis said, one summer even
  Together they did flow;
Their beams smiled sweetly
  In tenderness above,
And formed appropriately
  The radiant Star of Love!

There were two crystal streamlets
  In a valley side by side;
The music of their voices
  From each to each replied;
They listened to each other,
  And nearer, nearer came,
Till, in a gentle river,
  Their course became the same!

Two clouds, one Autumn evening,
  Lay cradled near the sun;
A sympathetic fervor
  Commingled them in one!—
With heaven's breath impelling,
  They traced the sun away,
And, like an angel's pinion,
  Bore to eternal day!

Such emblems nature giveth,
  For human hearts to view;
Why then, dear, should we slight tnem,
  And apart our paths pursue?—
One voice breathes through all things,—
  'Tis wrong to live alone!—
Oh! heed, my love, the lesson,
  And let our hearts be one!

REQUITED LOVE.

How rich and gushing through my heart
  The tide of passion flows !
What long-pent feelings stir and start !
  How bursts the folded rose !
No wilder dream of pride and bliss,
  Did e'er my life control,
Than now thy fond and fervid kiss
  Has wakened in my soul !

Oh, lady fair, thy form and face
  Are fashioned most divine,
And every charm and every grace
  And spell of love are thine !
Long had I knelt before thy feet,
  As Chaldean to his star,
But never dreamed thy love would greet
  My worship from afar !

But now I've held thee in my arms,—
  Close folded to my breast,—

With all thy radiant wealth of charms,—
I am supremely blest!
Not when the first-formed Beauty came
To Eden's morning bowers,
Knew earth a joy, or love a flame,
So rapturous as ours!

What bliss! what bliss! when to thy lips
Like fondling bees I clung,
And drank, in passions wild eclipse,
The honey of thy tongue!
My arms encircled thy sweet form,
As Grecia's golden waves
Did Venus, when, all fresh and warm,
She rose from ocean's caves!

Oh, man may be a God on earth,
In rapture and in pride,
When beings of celestial worth
Cling fondly to his side.
Queen of thy race! I feel it now,—
Olympian joy I feel,—
Since thou hast placed upon my brow
Affection's royal seal!

AT PARTING.

After a Family Bereavement.

How painful to me is this parting of sorrow !
  My heart yearns in anguish to turn from thy side.
No light will illumine my pathway to-morrow,
  But 'lone in its darkness mv soul must abide !

Though death has bereft me of all that was nearest,
  Some solace remained in the light of thy love :
Yet now, from my bosom, parts all that is dearest,
  And fades o'er the Deluge, the wing of the Dove !

Yet think not, in absence or grief I'll forget thee,
  Though now in the deepest despondence I go,
My heart has been thine since in rapture it met thee,
  'Tis now doubly thine in its anguish and woe !

My passion for thee is so strong and devoted,
  No change can remove from my bosom thy spell ;
O'er the stream of its joy thine image has floated,
  On the tide of its sorrow 'twill linger as well !

TO MARY.

" Oh purissima, oh bellissima,
Dulcis virgo Marie !"

While others sing for thee, sweet Mary,
  With songs as soft as lover's lute,
I, but a cold-toned visionary,
  Gaze on thy beauty, and am mute !—
I see thy charms before me pass,
Like fair birds o'er a lake's still glass,
  And feel them in my silent heart,
  Not shadows merely, but a part
Of my own spirit's dearest gems,
As jewels are a diadem's !

Had I a voice, young, gentle Mary,
  Could please thine ear, with joyous pride,
Like thine own musical Canary,
  I'd sing, enraptured by thy side !—
Like him, at dawn I'd charm thine ear,
At noon,—at dewy eve so dear,
  In dulcet numbers would I sing
  Thy virgin beauty's blossoming,—

And oh, though vain, would make my tone
Attempt the music of thine own !

But no, unequalled, beauteous Mary,
  I cannot breathe fit strains for thee,—
Thine eyes so bright,—thy form so faery,
  Demand superior minstrelsy !
Whene'er I gaze upon thy face,
With its expressive maiden grace,
  And list thy voice that sweetly flows,
  As fragrance from a spring-time rose,
My heart is touched,—my voice is still,—
Mute homage binds my daring will !

Yet still, entrancing, peerless Mary,
  I still can breathe for thee a prayer :
'May time thy beauty never vary,
  Nor shade thy brow with grief or care ;
May tears ne'er dim those smiling eyes,—
Those lips be never touched by sighs,—
  Thy barque float o'er a sunny sea,
  Mid isles of green and fragrancy,
And reach at last that Eden shore,
Where forms beloved have gone before !

A LADY'S VALENTINE.

Oh, years ago, we fondly met,
  With hearts elate, and hopes divine,
And pleasures in each bosom sate,
  Like angels in some pictured shrine;
Our brows were lit with smiles of youth,
  Our hearts were filled with mutual love;
Around us all seemed changeless truth,
  And cloudless skies were bright above,
No greater joy could then be mine,
Than to have been thy Valentine!

But years have passed—and fleeting time
  Has wrought a change in either lot;
My heart hath lost its dreams sublime,
  And thine those pleasant scenes forgot.
Thy feet have followed wealth and fame;
  Mine in a lowlier pathway gone;
Thine is a loved and honored name,
  While mine, alas! is all unknown.

Yet still my bosom yearns to thine,
And craves to be thy Valentine!

The bird that sings in vernal bowers,
  When all around is bright and blest,
Will still, in winter's gloomy hours,
  Wail sadly 'round its ruined nest:
And thus my heart, though thou art changed,
  And lost forever here to me,
Would prove its feelings unestranged,
  And fondly pour its song to thee.
Oh, then in dreams again be mine,
And own me as thy Valentine!

EPITAPHS.

On an Infant.

This little simple mound of earth
  Is for a double token given :
That here an *infant* had its birth,
  But now an *angel* dwells in heaven.

On an Aged Christian.

The grave, where so much goodness lies,
Is but a gateway to the skies,
Through which a saint has gone before,
And left us weeping at the door.

On a Young Man.

Though but a painful brief career,
  To him, on earth was given,
Yet, mourner, dry the gushing tear,
  He's passed to peace, in heaven.
How blest the fortunes of the young,
  Who thus, ere age can wither,
Hear sweetly, from the Saviour's tongue,
  The mandate,—"Come up hither!"

THE DAY OF FREEDOM.

A POEM

Pronounced at Tuscaloosa, Alabama,

JULY 4, 1838.

TO

HON. WILLIAM RUSSELL SMITH,

OF ALABAMA,

THIS TRIBUTE IN EARLY LIFE

IS AGAIN INSCRIBED,

BY HIS FRIEND,

THE AUTHOR.

POEM.

If it be good to think on virtues past,—
If many a noble secret, rich and true,
On history's pictured page, neglected lies,
From which the heart might sage instruction glean,
And a sweet moral learn, to guide its path,
Through times bewildering labyrinths, aright,—
If the brave deeds, by patriot sires achieved,
When viewed again, their children hap'ly prompt
To emulation pure, and thus inspire
A kindred spirit, and a genial love,—
A gratitude ennobling to the heart,—
Oh, sure it must be good and right alway,
To nurse the memories of this sacred day!

Illustrious Sabbath of a ransomed race!
With swelling hearts, we hail thy glorious dawn!
What proud emotions fill our breasts with joy,—
What songs triumphant tremble on our tongues,—
What gracious memories of ancestral worth—
Of hero deed—of patriot wisdom—rise,—
With sacred forms, enrobed in glory's folds,
What heavenly mien, like kingly spectres, pass,
In staid procession, over memory's eye,—
And, oh, what visions proudly thrilling come,
Of our blest country's future destinies,—
As we, once more, thy rapturous advent greet,
Morn of the free, the virtuous, and the great!

Earth hath her eras,—many a noble one,—
The loved memorials of exalted deed,—
Her trophied anniversaries of fame,—
Kings have their festivals of pomp and power,—
Nations their triumphs for some victor-field,—
But ne'er, since time his monarch-march began,
Has day more glorious, ever dawned o'er earth,
Or shed the breath of Heaven, on hearts, whose pulse,
To music's tone, with sympathetic thrill,

Kept prouder time,—than this propitious morn!—
This sacred day, when Freedom, rudely driven
By grim oppression, from the orient world,
Found, 'mid the bowers of the rosy West,
A shrine and temple where her head might rest!

Auspicious morn!—when our forefathers dared
Despite the leagued artilleries of power,
And in the wonder of a startled world,
Proclaim, they were of right, and would be free!
And to mankind, displayed that glorious chart,
Whose sentiments sublime, this day, have dimmed
Bright eyes, with pearls of gratitude and joy!—
This Bible of their faith, whose burning words
Were sacrilegious deemed by nations then,
But whose eternal principles and truths,
Upon the wings of every wind, have sped
O'er earth,—'till, on their thrones, have tyrants felt
Their sceptres trembling, like storm-shaken leaves,
At winter's touch,—and they themselves have quaked,
As Judea's Ruler, when the Apostle spoke,
Before its "still, small voice,"—so just and true!
Immortal Instrument!—whose starry light,

So dim and tremulous at first, has shed
A rosier glow, o'er man's terrestrial lot,
Than,—since the Primal Fall, save that blest gift,
Brought by the Paraclete,—from heaven e'er fell!
Well might celestial voices, by night,
With harps star-tuned and brimmed with melody,
To thy sad children, on their hills, have sung
Thy glad apostleship, and cried in joy,—
"Good will to man, and Liberty on earth!"

Such thoughts, the bard, not sacrilegious, deems.
For oh, if heaven's directing hand e'er-traced
Its lineaments of glory, on the deeds
Of mortal man, or wreathed a favoring smile
Of its approval, 'mid the dimmer lights,
That emanate from mere terrestrial power,—
Its finger and its rays have left their glow,
And impress, on Columbia's history!
Else how could that small patriot band,—
Our valiant sires—with but an infant's panoply—
With Britain's power successfully have striven,
And from its culmination proud, torn down
The lion-banner of St. George, and trailed

Its trophied glories in th' ensanguined dust!—
Else how, when storm and darkness gathered o'er
The land, and serried hosts, multudinous,
Like Vandal conquerors, came, th' inglorious strife
To consummate, base Avarice had begun,—
Could the frail barque, triumphant, o'er the waves
Of the vexed sea, been borne in safety on?—
Or our loved sires, above the cloud, beheld
The starry emblem of success and hope,—
Like that, new-born, the Eastern Magi, led,—
Serenely bright, a comforter and guide,
Through doubt and trouble, till their raptured eyes
Upon their wished for Deity reposed!
Else how, to them, could such prophetic dreams—
Such sweet assurances,—'mid penury,
And strife, and lean-eyed famine and distress,—
Of future power and glory, have been given,
As cheered their hearts, and succored their sad hopes,
In stern bereavement's darkest—lonelicst hour,—
And made them utter, then, glad strains, like *this*,—
Poured from the lips of one, with prescient power,
When, down the vista of the opening years,
Like Scotia's Seer, at Sunset's time, he saw
Afar, the grand results of that great Day,

Whose Anniversary we now have met,—
In proud fulfilment of his glowing words,—
Beneath this sacred dome—God's templed shrine—
With echoing hearts, to celebrate:

Oh, it shall be a glorious day,*
  Renowned in fame and story,—
When we are sleeping in our graves,
  'Twill live in deathless glory!
Our children's children long shall greet
  Its glad return, with swelling bosoms,
And on its advent proudly meet,
  To twine for us fame's fadeless blossoms!
With pomp of drum,—with bugle note,—
  With bonfires brightly blazing,—
With cannon roar,—with martial throngs,—
  Their eagle-banners raising!
With shout, and song, and dance, and glee,
  And bright illuminations,—
They'll hail the Sabbath of the Free,
  Through unborn generations!

* A paraphraso of John Adams' celebrated letter to his wife, dated Philadelphia, July 5, 1776, which Mr. Webster has so eloquently elaborated in one of his orations.

I speak not wild, ideal words,—
  The brood of fancy's vision—
I know that only by our swords,
  We'll win the boon Elysian!
I know the toil and strife and blood,—
  The loss of life and treasure,—
'Twill cost us to maintain these States,
  And consummate this measure,—
Yet, through the gloom around us now,—
  The clouds impending o'er ye,—
The storm, the strife, the battle smoke,
  I see the rays of glory!—
And though this strife may last us long,—
  Though you and I may rue it,—
The deed is done,—and foes, in vain,
  Will struggle to undo it!—
We, we may die,—die vassal slaves,—
  Perhaps inglorious perish,—
Yet, yet our children, o'er our graves,
  Will freedom's altar cherish!—
And oft with song, and dance, and glee,
  And bright illuminations,—
They'll hail the Sabbath of the Free,
  Through unborn generations!

Prophetic words !—Oh, ne'er did favoring heaven,
To Israel's weeping Bard, rapt and inspired,
Serener visions give,—'mid exiled grief,—
Of widowed Zion's god-like triumphs, when
His wailing harp from Babel's Stream he snatched,
And on the trembling air, the voice of song,
Divinely threw,—than thus, upon the gaze
Of young Columbia's Brave and Eloquent,
Flashed with benignant light, bright as the wings
Of Cherubim, through sunset's gates, beheld,
At summer-eve, when clustering angels come
With plumes all fire, to watch the Day-God greet
His Ocean-bride,—and their divinity
Breathed on his lips, until his word became
A consolation and a promise sweet,—
Like some young angel singing in the dark,—
Through the grim storm-time of their gloom and strife,—
The hearts of Liberty's young pioneers
To cheer !

And nobler, grander, was the boon,—
The gracious benison, so kindly given,—
Than the enthusiasts dreamed. No felon death,—

No ignominious fate, awaited them,—
The brave forefathers of the Free !—They saw
The blessed consummation of their hopes,—
They saw the stricken eagle rise again,—
Shake, from his tattered plumes, the dust of strife,—
Soar in the gold of an unclouded heaven,—
And, with a scream of mingled joy and pride,
Place the effulgent Standard of the Stars,
High on the parapets of fame. They saw
Their land beloved,—the Canaan of their hearts,—
Their El Dorado realized,—revive !—
Its cottage homes in peace and plenty smile,—
The rosy children prattling at the door,—
The mother singing at her wheel within !—
Its sea like-fields with snowy harvests teem,—
Its genial sky, with storms no more be dimmed,
But blue as beauty's eye, bend o'er their heads,—
Saw Virtue, Science, Opulence, and Peace,–
The roseate muses of the Grecian Dream,
Linked in the Flower Dance of their vernal prime,—
With prodigality, their treasures, spread
O'er all the land ;—beheld its realm extend
Wide as the wings of light,—o'er ocean's wave,—
O'er mountains pinnacled in clouds,—o'er plains

As kingdoms broad, where nature's veil had hung,
Unlifted since the birth of Time ;—and saw
The citadel, which they had reared, become
The home and refuge of th' oppressed and sad
Of every clime,—until all tongues confessed,
In all its hours of pageantry and pomp,
No monument the world had ever seen,
Of man, so glorious and so grand as theirs,—
The moral Parthenon of Liberty !

Such was thy lot, oh PROPHET ORATOR
Whose tongue foretold the glories of this Day !
And his, that other patriarch, whose renown
Must live co-eval with our country's fame,—
The immortal PENMAN of this glorious Chart !
Like sacred brothers, side by side, ye bore
The Ark of Freedom, through the stormy sea !
United heart and hand, in that good cause,—
Its tribulation, and its triumph too,—
Ye each beheld, upon your country's brow,
The coronal of freedom,—each, in turn,
Was called, by grateful millions, to rule o'er
The land, in peace, which ye had saved in war !

And then,—when ye had seen, full realized,
Your fondest wishes,—full your fame,—*even then*,—
On this illustrious morn, amid the shout
Of congregating millions, whose glad hearts
Were brimmed with gratitude and love, for you,—
With freedom's music rolling on your ears,—
The last sounds of the fading earth,—and oh,
While "Independence" trembled on your lips,—
Your spirits passed, in union, unto God!

Oh, if the observant heart of man has e er,
Amid His works, the influence aweing, felt
Of the O'er-Ruling Power, or recognized
His interference in the affairs of earth,—
His palpable assurances of love,—
The angel pinion flashing through the cloud,—
It must behold it, in a scene like that,—
When twin Elijahs seek at once the sky,—
Dropping their robes all luminious with stars,—
Amid a nation's kindred panoplies,
Unsoiled and glittering in their birthday light,
And all Columbia's sons in reverence bow,
With quivering lips, and tearful eyes, and own
The immediate workings of the Almighty God!

Oft hath the story of Columbia's fame,—
Her infant struggles, and her proud success,—
Her scenes of suffering and of victory,—
By lips more touched with fire than mine, been told!
My harp, unused to soar in epic strains,
Is far too faint her glories to recount.
But long will Eloquence and Song enwreathe,
To celebrate her early deeds. Even now,—
Through all the broad expanse of this green land,—
From many a sunlit mount, and shaded vale,—
From learning's shrines, and fair religion's domes,—
A thousand voices swell her history,
And many a fervid lip, with music tone,—
In sweet remembrance of those blessed times,—
And proud commemoration of this Day,—
Pours forth some patriot lyric such as *this:*

Freemen!—rise and hail the morn,
When Columbia's flag was borne
Proudly o'er a tyrant's scorn,
By the Brave and Free!
Rise, for 'tis the glorious day,
When your fathers, from the sway
Of oppression, tore away
Hope and Liberty!

Long and bloody was the strife,—
Feerlessly they perilled life,—
Daring e'en the savage knife,
For the glorious prize!
But the God of battles, then,
Battled with those valiant men,
And the Bow of Peace, agen
Gladdened patriot eyes!

Sound! then sound the plausive strain,—
Shout! oh, shout, from mount to plain,
And, with rapture, hail, again,
Freedom's natal day!
Let the deep-toned cannon tell,
And the pealing clarion swell,
Joyfully, the tyrant's knell,
On our Jubilee!

God of Nations!—unto thee,
Grateful, now we bend the knee,
For our peace and liberty,
And our country's fame!
Guard!—oh guard!—our nation's cause,—
Shield our rights, direct our laws,

And, for all our vaunted joys,
We will praise thy name!

Though often thus have Poetry and Love,
Their tributes laid at fair Columbia's feet—
Though many a heaven-tuned tongue has, on this day,
Her triumphs, told in burning words, until
The patriot eye has filled with sudden tears,
And the stern heart has felt its fountains heaved,
In mingling gratitude, and pride, and joy,—
As lift the waters of the moon-led sea,
Beneath the smilings of Endymion's bride;—
Yet ne'er by Sage, or Orator, or Bard,
Have I e'er heard, our Country's story told
So eloquent, as from the wither'd lips
Of some old Soldier of her Battle-Time!
Oh, I have listened at the twilight hour,
When evening's shades seemed blending with the light
Of by-gone years, and, softly on the heart,
The grateful dews of memory distilled,
As, bent beneath accumulated years,
With time's white blossoms 'mid his ringlets wreathed,

His mouldered tongue has told, of those dark days
Of peril and of blood,—and I have seen
Th' extinguished fire of battle and of youth
Once more flash in his palsied eyes, and gleam
Effulgent, round his scar-seamed brow, as he
Has pictured forth those scenes of suffering,
And wrong,—the wretchedness, and pain, and want,—
The valiant deeds, too small for history's pen,
But oh, full worthy of immortal fame,
Our patriot sires achieved and bore, to win
The glorious privileges we possess!
And, as I've gazed upon the plain, old man,
And child-like listened to him, I have felt
A reverence,—not earth's famed emperors,
Her titled princes, or her lineal lords,—
Descendants of a dateless ancestry,—
Enrobed in all their pomp and gorgeousness,—
Could raise,—and, in the fullness of my heart,
Have cried—God's blessings on the old man's head!

And such a one, I lately knew, who dwelt
Not far remote from here. Though but a boy,
When conflict's pinions overspread our land,
And though the strife raged deadliest round his home,

Making strong hearts to quail, and aged men
To tremble, he unfearingly went forth,
To meet the invader's fiery wrath, and drive
His minions from the soil. Valorously
He bore himself, and, with his youthful arm,
Chivalrous deeds performed, which, in a land
Of legendary lore, had placed his name,
Embalmed in song,—beside the hallowed ones
Of Douglas and of Percy! And not unsung
Entirely is his fame. Romance hath wreathed,
With flowery fingers and with wizard art,
That hangs the votive chaplet on the heart,—
His story, 'mid her fictions, and hath given
His name and deeds, to after time. When last
This trophied anniversary came round,
And called Columbia's patriot children out,
To greet its advent,—*the old man was here,*—
Serenely smiling as an Autumn sun
Just dropping down the golden West, to seek
Its evening couch. Few months agone, I saw
Him, in his peaceful home, with all around,
Its wishes could demand,—and, by his side,
The loved companion of his youthful years,—
This singing maiden of his boyhood's time,—

She who had cheered him, with her smiles, when
clouds
Were o'er his country's prospects,—who had trod,
In sun and shade, life's devious paths with him,
And whom kind heaven had still preserved, to bless,
With all the fullness of maternal wealth,
The mellowing afternoon of his decline !
Where now are they ?—the old man and his wife !
Alas ! the broadening sun sets in the night,—
The ripened shock falls on the reaper's arm,—
The lingering guest must leave the hall at last,—
The music ceases when the feast is done.—
The old man and his wife are gone !—from earth
Have passed in peace to heaven ! and summer's
flowers—
Beneath the light of this triumphal day,—
Luxuriant sweets, are shedding o'er
Th' unsculptured grave of HORSE-SHOE ROBINSON !*
Thus pass the seasons—thus earth's pomps—
and thus
Have well-nigh all the patriarchs of our land,

---

*James Robinson, the hero of Mr. Kennedy's admirable historic novel, died near Tuscaloosa, Alabama, April 28th. 1838, aged seventy eight years.

The proud memorials of our valor's time,
Star-like descended from our sky and sank
'Neath the horizon's rim. But oh! they rise
In glory as they fade from us!—and burn
In constellations with celestial bands!
Few, few survive! The gently heaving turf,—
So mutely eloquent,—so touching, yet so still,—
In many an unfenced graveyard, marks their rest!
No pillared cenotaph is theirs,—no shrine,—
No Kaaba,—where pilgrims may resort,—
The exiled pilgrims of each suffering clime,—
The holocausts of memory, to pay.
A nobler monument is theirs, than such!—
It is around them,—'tis their country's fame!
Behold it in the blessings we enjoy,—
The liberty and peace that smiles on all
They fought for,—and the opulence that robes,
With more than orient magnificence,
The land they rescued,—and behold it too,
In yon proud flag,—fair freedom's metaphor!—
That waves triumphant, with increasing stars,
On every sea, beneath the engirdling sun,
That man has visited, or Commerce won!

These glorious benisons, they gave to us,
Are their best monuments,—and shall we not,
In all its purity, the boon protect ?—
Shall we, degenerate from our fathers' worth,
Forget the lessons, they so nobly taught,
By deed as well as word ?—Shall we permit
Their legacy,—our children's hope,—to fail—
And demon Tyranny again to wave
His raven banner, o'er our prostrate land ?
Forbid it heaven ! Shades of the mighty dead,—
Our country's canonized sires,—forbid !

Far other, on this consecrated day,
Rapt fancy deems will be Columbia's lot !—
The heart, elate with patriot fire, and filled
With holiest memories, like swarming bees,
Pictures bright Edens, on the Future's page,—
Until th' enthusiast Hope, moon-eyed and fond,
Becomes a prophecy ! Oh, if the light,
Olympian, that encircled ancient bards,—
Making the names of Poet and of Prophet one,—
Had not *now* faded,—what ecstatic beams,
Far shining from immortal Freedom's sun,—
Through a long vista of impending years,—

Might not now gladden our bewildered eyes !
Alas, that light has fled,—that lyre is hushed !
But sweet assurances,—more doubly sure,
Than weird prophetic tongue,—to us remain !—
He who upbore us through our infant strife,—
And guides us still, hath said,—that, " as we sow,
Our sons shall reap !"—*Our fate is with ourselves !*
And oh, if we observe the noble lessons taught,—
To guide us,—by our sainted fathers' lips,—
If we inherit aught of that pure fire,
Which burnt, on Freedom's shrine—that vestal flame,
Whose going-out will be our country's fall,—
If, with a lidless jealousy, we guard
The open portals of our sacred fane,—
Alike from strange and parricidal hand,—
And oh, still more, if, with regardful eye,
We look,—it is no bigot lip that speaks,
Nor sacrilegious yet, though stained with sin,—
In homage up to Him, our Fathers' God,—
Columbia's star-roofed citadel shall stand,
Free and unshaken till the death of Time !—
With all her prospects bright and beautiful,
As is the signet Bow of Hope and Love,
Upon the Future's lifting cloud to-day !

'Tis not for me, those lessons to repeat,
Or sage instructions, on this day, to give.
Tongues, to whose music, hoar experience,
A deeper wisdom, than belongs to mine,
Has given, and, a more searching lore, has brought,—
Who better know, 'neath what deceptive waves,
The sands and shallows lie, that shipwreck States,—
Would more befit the counsels of this hour.
But yet some lessons, I have learned,—some truths,—
Which my brief wanderings, in the ways of men,
Have more impressed upon a watchful mind,
Than book, or scroll, or many pictured verse !
And, though they may appear but trite, to most,
To me, they seem, fraught with instruction good,
And wholesome, to the patriot heart.

Take one.—

Beware of party strife !—It is the bane,
That blights and poisons many a goodly State.
It is the apple, envying discord threw
In Beauty's bower, and withered all its peace !—
The tempting snake, that trailed its festering slime,
O'er Eden's buds, and poured its mildew breath
Upon the loveliest of our race,—the sinless Eve,—

The incarnation sweet of innocence
And purity,—th' embodied poetry
Of light and love !—Beware of Party strife !
By it have all free nations fallen. With brow
Of light, and innocence, and smiles,—and mien,
So like to virtuous Liberty and Thought,
That oft the free, confiding mind mistakes
The semblance for the God himself,—it wears,
Beneath its shining garb, a scorpion's heart,—
And breathes pollution, like a leper touch !
It is the subtlest foe of private peace,—
Frost to domestic love,—and fire to friendship's
bonds !
Oh, could you watch its gradual progress through
The human heart,—and see it change the young,
The buoyant, and the pure, by its fell shade,
Into the stern, the envious, and the cold,—
Th' unshadowed brow, into the haughty frown,—
And wreathe, around the chaste and loving lip,
The sneer of scorn,—oh, you would turn, and curse
Its treacherous image, for a fiend,—and swear
For aye to bruise its serpent head. It wends
Its way into the Statesman's breast, and makes,
By the Circéan influence of its spell,

His lofty mind, bow down to lowly thought,—
His eagle-wing stoop from its Alpine flight,—
Until, in utter selfishness, his heart
Forgets his nobler purposes, and bends,
In vile subservience, at *its* shrine. By it,
The patriot citizen, too oft, is driven,
Into the paths of error, and uplifts
A recreant hand, against the government,
His fathers nourished with their heart's best blood!
Oh, then, beware of Party strife!

There is
Another lesson, we, this day, should learn:—
To love alike all portions of our land!
The human heart is full of selfishness!—
Those whom it knew in youth, it loves the best—
The spot, where first it saw the morning sun
Lift o'er the eastern trees, is dearest aye—
The scenes around its residence become
A part of its existence, and it deems
The fragrant air above the neighboring hills,—
The gurgling streamlet in the sylvan vale,—
The green-rimmed lake,—the sweet sky overhead,—
The whispering trees,—are kindred with its veins!

And this is right !—But we should never let
Contracted selfishness, our feelings, sway.
The mind should give its pinions to the heart,
And teach its gushing sympathies to spread
O'er all the land,—from farthest Maine, to where,
Above a lately ransomed realm, the Star
Of a young empire glistens in the South !

Though broad and almost boundless is our land,—
Yet, o'er it all, can the reflecting mind
Associations meet, to make it love
Alike each part. *One common cause is ours !*—
The glorious cause of Human Liberty !—
The same remembrances and gratitude,—
One common hope,—one undivided love !—
The same sweet tongue our mutual fathers spoke,—
Its graceful literature, its rising lore !—
The same blood leaping through our veins,—and, oh,—
Emblem of this, and more than this,—one love,—
One common worship, for this festal day !

What, though each Star that on our banner shines,

Moves in its orbit with a sovereign sway,—
With laws, with institutions of its own,—
Yet 'round one common centre all converge,
And each, upon its golden pathway, wheels
With sympathetic harmony and force
And equipoise sublime. Strike but one orb
From its appointed place, or rudely dim
Its purity and light, and soon the whole
Great frame-work of the sky, would madly whirl
In dire confusion and disaster vast,
A wreck to make even Heaven's high angels grieve!
Stars of the East!—New England's Pleiades!
Shine on—in light unshadowed shine!—
And guide new Pilgrims to your Rock of Faith—
Your war-crowned hills, and rich historic plains,
Where Freedom's feet first trod the tyrant down,
And left their imprints, never more to fade!
And oh, ye Planets of the roseate West!
Bright-eyed as Vesper with her lamp of love!—
Or radiant Mercury, or red-browed Mars:—
Gild your vast plains with fertilizing rays,
Till need-born empires start to civic life,
Where late the sandalled chief or bison trod
O'er prairied deserts, or by endless streams!

Even now, brave hearts, by high heroic deeds,
Have won your welcome, in the throng of States,
The golden Galaxy by freemen framed!
And oh, may heaven, from each attuning sphere,
Long breathe the music of congenial faith,
Of Union, fellowship and kindred love.
For, States fraternal, ye are all but One!
Each purpled page that tells your warrior deeds,
Each name sublime, that glows among your gems,
Each work of Art that wealth and beauty brings,
Each burning song by native minstrel sung,
All, all belong to fair Columbia's fame—
Are treasured trophies of her blended power,—
The gemmed regalia of her kingless realm!
And whilst we love, each one his native spot,
As best and brightest of all parts of earth,
Still should the heart, with patriotic glow,
Cling to all sections of this glorious Land!

Such were his feelings, an untutored bard,
Who *thus*, in a rude lay, his homage breathed
Unto *his* native home,—and flung the gift,
Like a wild-flower, upon her breast:

I.

Land of the South !—imperial land !—
  How proud thy mountains rise !—
How sweet thy scenes on every hand !
  How fair thy covering skies !
But not for this,—oh, not for these,
  I love thy fields to roam,—
Thou hast a dearer spell to me,—
  Thou art my native home !

II.

Thy rivers roll their liquid wealth,
  Unequalled to the sea,—
Thy hills and valleys bloom with health,
  And green with verdure be !
But, not for thy proud ocean streams,
  Not for thine azure dome,—
Sweet, sunny South !—I cling to thee,—
  Thou art my native home !

III.

I've stood beneath Italia's clime,
  Beloved of tale and song,—

On Helvyn's hills, proud and sublime,
Where nature's wonders throng;
By Tempe's classic sunlit streams,
Where Gods, of old, did roam,—
But ne'er have found so fair a land
As thou—my native home!

IV.

And thou hast prouder glories too,
Than nature ever gave,—
Peace sheds o'er thee, her genial dew,
And Freedom's pinions wave,—
Fair science flings her pearls around,
Religion lifts her dome,—
These, these endear thee, to my heart,—
My own, loved native home!

V.

And "heaven's best gift to man" is thine,—
God bless thy rosy girls!—
Like sylvan flowers, they sweetly shine,—
Their hearts are pure as pearls!

And grace and goodness circle them,
  Where'er their footsteps roam,—
How can I then, whilst loving them,
  Not love my native home!

VI.

Land of the South!—imperial land!—
  Then here's a health to thee,—
Long as thy mountain barriers stand,
  May'st thou be blest and free!—
May dark dissension's banner ne'er
  Wave o'er thy fertile loam,—
But should it come, there's one will die,
  To save his native home!

But now my strains must cease. Freemen and friends,
Too long I hold you with my song.—But yet
My lyre, rude as it is, hath, heart-like, caught
The inspiration of this hour, and fain
Would linger on its theme! It cannot be!
Time wanes,—another Anniversary
Will soon be with the past! But oh, as this,
To heaven conveys the anthems of the free!—

As now our country stands, robed in a light,
By Grecian pomp or Roman fame unreached,
Her people happy, and her laws supreme,—
As o'er her realm, science and happiness
Prevail,—so may she stand to greet, with joy,
Full many a dawn of this beloved day !—
And oh, when Time shall fold his wing, and lay
His sceptre down, and, king-like, go to rest,—
May fair Columbia's temple still be seen,
Untarnished, and entire—unwrent and free—
The last spot of the crumbling world, to fall,—
Its spires amid the stars,—the smiling stars,—
Its basis earth,—its canopy the sky !

THE NUPTIAL FÉTE.

AN IRREGULAR POEM.

TO —— OF ALABAMA.

Here is a frail memorial of a festive occasion, to the happiness of which, both by your beauty and gayety, you were one of the chief contributors. Will the Muse, who inspired the production, give it her smiles ?

March, 1841.

THE NUPTIAL FÊTE.

I.

How proudly, o'er the yielding waters,
  Our gallant Steamer speeds along !—
Fairest and first of Fulton's daughters,—
  The queen of all the goodly throng !

Before her prow, the liquid mirror,—
  Glass of the wild-duck and the sky,—
Breaks into ripples, as in terror
  The foaming spoiler hurries by !

On either hand the trees receding,
  Seem moving quickly up the stream,
And hill and dale and field succeeding,
  Pass by, like pictures in a dream !

The river too, the noble river,
  Like some bright serpent, winds along;
And never was a lovelier, never,
  Renowned by bard in olden song!

Ah, had the days of Nymph and Naiad,—
  Sweet creatures of the Grecian dream!—
Not vanished, like the fabled Pleiad,
  What forms would haunt this sylvan stream!

Then oft at noon, wild song and laughter
  Would ring from out her beechen creeks,
And merry shouts come pealing after,
  Of half-seen spirits at their freaks!

But now alas, all's calm and quiet,
  Save where yon Steamer holds her way;
There mirth and song and festive riot
  Mingle their giddy roundelay!

Lo! from her deck, her painted streamer,
  Floats forth upon the fresh'ning breeze;
And wreaths and banners!—you would deem her
  Some fairy barque on fairy seas!

And softly too !—what sounds of pleasure
  Are ringing from her peopled side !
The drum and flute, with gladsome measure,
  And violin, are all allied !

Ah, well may music's bells be ringing,
  And well that Boat be deck'd in state ;
A gallant party she is bringing
  To celebrate a NUPTIAL FETE.

II.

Change we the scene ; our numbers change,
And view a picture bright and strange.
Within that Steamer's halls we stand—
How fair the scene, how rich and grand !
Oh, ne'er did orient palace shine
In workmanship more near divine !—
Rich tapestries from India's loom,
Purple and gold, bedeck the room—
Gay curtains shed a softened gloom,
That gloom which sways and wins the heart
In passion's hour, and seems a part,
Almost, of that deep tenderness

Which only loving hearts possess!
Art's richest miracles are here;—
Trophies to fame and memory dear:
Lo! from yon wall a GUIDO shines,—
These are his own immortal lines.
Look on that face!—never was given
To earth a brow more lit from heaven!—
So high, so calm, so pure and sweet,
We almost worship at her feet,—
Hailing, with deep devotion's breath,
The Virgin Mother of our Faith!

But turn from this: yon sculptured form
Appears with life instinct and warm!—
Ah, 'tis a model of that Dream,—
The Warrior-Poet's sweetest theme,—
Who well its peerless grace portrayed—
"The sun in human limbs arrayed!"
And many a bust you here may see
Of names embalmed in history.
Behold this brow: how meekly grand!—
He was the Father of this Land!—
And oh, till fades time's latest sun,
Shall live the name of WASHINGTON!

And when the last faint star of Eve
Shall o'er our Country's relics grieve,
Some lingering bard beneath its rays,
Shall still his matchless merit praise ![*]

III.

Such decorations meet the eye,
Where'er it turns entranced around ;
But oh, a double witchery,
The senses, holds in thraldom bound :
For lofty mirrors, ranged between,
Reduplicate the lovely scene !—
Mirrors as bright as that which won
The gaze of Liriope's son,—
The world's most famed and beauteous one,—
Showing his features all so fair
Until, fond youth, he perished there !—
Or clear as that calm crystal wave,
  Which our first Mother's heart beguiled,
As back her charms it sweetly gave,
  While, o'er her shoulder, Angels smiled !—

* The festivities here recorded, took place on the birth-day of the "Father of his Country."

And ever since that witching time,—
So, cynic bards have told in rhyme,—
Her daughters all have lover to look
On parlor-glass, or mirroring brook,
And, like their Mother, blessed the view,
And thought that they saw Angels too !

These lofty mirrors range the halls,
And hide the Cabin's narrow walls,
So that its bounds no more appear
  The limits of an earthly scene,
But some gay tent spread in the air,
  For fairies bright to revel in !

IV.

Such is the scene : but who art these
That hold their festive revelries ?—
Behold, slow winding through the room,
To merry fife and throbbing drum,
What crowds in gay procession come !
First gorgeous banners meet the sight,
Half-flashing in the softened light !

Now gallant soldiers make their way;
A goodly and a brave array !—
What lofty plumes nod on the eye !—
How brightly gleams the musketry !—
How proudly up the hall they march,
Beneath its decorated arch !—
Shoulder to shoulder on they come,
While quicker rolls the rattling drum !—
Whoever saw a nobler band !—
The soldiers of our native land !—
And though no foeman's summons rude
Hath called them now to fields of blood,—
To hasten, as their father's erst
Upon the invading Britons burst,—
  And though in only sportive part,
To hail a comrade's nuptial day,—
  A Brother dear to every heart,—
Their length'ning lines they now display;
Yet who can look on their array,
Nor feel his pulses quicker play,
No feel his country's rights alway,
Shall safe from foreign rapine stay,
While shielded by her forest men,
Each one a Soldier-Citizen !

And now within the hall they stand,
Their lines arrayed on either hand:
Silent is music's swelling sound;
Not stiller stand the statues round!

V.

But lo! what brilliant visions come,
Beneath the portals of the room!
  Glows not the air with added light?—
Do not the mirrors brighter blaze?—
  Is't not some magic wins the sight?—
Have kindlier planets lent their rays?—
Look where they come!—ah no, 'tis real,—
No vision from the realm ideal!—
These are the maidens of our land,—
  Sure, lovelier creatures never shone on earth!—
Sweet Alabama's daughters, bland
  And fair, as the fair clime that gave them birth!

VI.

Our Southern women!—You may talk
  Of Saxon beauties by the score,

Their sculptured forms, their queenly walk,
  Their charms renowned on every shore ;
Of famed Italia's glowing daughters,
  Voluptuous as their country's fruits,
Their eyes as soft as shadowed waters,
  Their songs as sweet as Angels' flutes ;
Of Grecian Maidens fair as those
  By old Anacreon's numbers sung ;
Of Harem beauties that repose
  Like pearls in some dark casket flung :
Yet, if you once will gaze with me,—
  Your bosom tuned for beauty's call,—
You'll own that though divine *they* be,
  Our Southern women beat them all !

VII.

Now winding on, the maidens come,
  To music's most ecstatic measure ;
Sweet flowers upon their foreheads bloom,
  Their soft eyes beam with pleasure !
As brightly down the hall they move,
Breathes 'round an atmosphere of love ;

Each soldier doffs his martial plume,
And Valor honors Beauty's bloom!
On still they come, and still they glance
Like angels in a prophet's trance!
But hark, a softer strain is heard!
Is that the warbling of a bird?—
A sweeter voice was ne'er by music stirred!—

1.

Strew your flowers, blushing flowers,
  Strew them at their feet;
Strew your flowers, in rosy showers,
  Offerings bright and sweet!

2.

Wave your banners, gorgeous banners,
  Wave them in their pride;
The bride now comes, the beauteous bride,
  With the bridegroom at her side!

3.

Last eve beheld their nuptials sweet,
  Last eve they formed the tie divine,

And now with smiling friends they meet,
  In festive mood 'round pleasure's shrine!

4.

Then strew your flowers, your banners wave,
  And hail them as they come;—
Oh, may their skies be ever bright,
  And joy around them bloom!

VIII.

Through the portals now they enter,
  Love's selected, favored pair;
In the bride all beauties centre,
  Fairest of the many fair!
O'er her brow what blushes speeding,
  Whisper more than words can tell,
Of the truth and joy exceeding,
  That her lovely bosom swell!
Young and fair and sinless creature!
  Life to her has all been love!—
Peerless form, and radiant feature,—
  Fair as Dian's snowy dove!

Ever 'mid bright flowers straying,
 Has her pathway hither been,
Birds 'mid blossoms 'round her playing,—
 Angel-guarded from all sin!—
Now in all her youthful dreaming,—
 Like a young moon in the sky,
On love's heaven softly beaming,—
 Hath she pledged her faith for aye!
Oh, this world has many pleasures,
 Kindly showered from above,
But of all its Eden treasures,
 None so sweet as plighted love!

IX.

And who is he, the favored one,
Who thus this beauteous bride has won?—
See him proudly by her standing,
Form erect, and brow commanding,
Oh, what hope, what peerless bliss!
What dreams celestial, now are his!
Many a wreath has crowned his brow,
Life's dearest one is on it now!—
For, what is wealth, or what is fame,
Or what Ambition's laurelled name?—

Although their songs may fire the breast,
With a dreaming and unrest,
Will not,—cannot be supprest!
Without love, man's earliest thrall,—
The Eve that never knew a fall!—
The Nymph that dwells from courts apart
Yet soothes the Numa of the heart!
That love is his: and proudly now
Its radiance decks his manly brow.
It well befits him too, for he
Has won the trophy worthily!
Oh, if the precious boon of woman's love,—
  The star for which we yearn through life,
The leaf brought by the ark-returning dove,
  The rainbow o'er a world of strife,—
Fitly belongs to any, 'tis to such
As feel most deep the magic of her touch,—
'Tis to those souls, where genius—spark of heaven—
Shines with the glory of its native levin!

X.

And such the bridegroom: though the leaves
  Of youth have scarcely lost their dew,

Yet that pure light, which fame achieves,
  Is brightening now their fading hue:
For he in learning's paths hath trode,
Hath plucked the flowers along the road,
Hath twined her garlands round his name,
And proudly won a Poet's fame!—
And she, now blushing by his side,
Is,—sweetest name on Earth!—a Poet's Bride!

XI.

Oh, had the Bard, who faintly sings
  These gladsome nuptials now,
But half the music on his strings,
  But half the wild poetic glow,
That unto SYLVAN's muse belongs,
  He'd wake a glad, mellifluous strain,—
The sweetest of our Southern songs,—
  In honor of the wedded twain!—
For oh, when Beauty, Genius weds,
The fairest flowers should deck their heads,
The brightest buds of song should twine
A garland for the bridal shrine,
And music pour its sweetest tide,
In tribute to a Poet's Bride!

XII.

A POET'S BRIDE !—what visions come,
  Like bright birds soaring, at the word,
What pictures light my lonely room,
  From the long past, by memory stirred !—
They come, they come, and now they pass,
Like shadows, over old Agrippa's glass !

Lo ! standing 'neath Italian skies,
I see a laurelled Bard arise !
'Tis he, whose songs, all songs above,
Have hymned the gentle powers of love.
Beside him leans a youthful form
With all love's sweet perfections warm !
Around his neck, her bright arms wreathing,
What whispers in his ear are breathing !
She smiles, and, kindling at the smile,
He wakes his minstrelsy the while !
Oh, all his songs are dear to fame,
And LAURA lives with PETRARCH'S name !*

* In this, as in two of the succeeding instances, so much regard is not had to those who were united in "the holy estate of matrimony," as to those who were indissolubly associated in poetic interest,—who were wedded in soul and feeling, as in fame.

Another scene—Broad halls are shining,
  Filled with fashion's sparkling throng ;
Bridal garlands they are twining
  For a favored son of song !—
And beside him, leaning, trembling,
In her grace a fawn resembling,
  Is the gentle one that long
Hath held his heart in homage bound !
Now his wishes she has crowned,
And the sweetest boon of heaven,
To Erin's Patriot-Minstrel, given !
But the visions quicker pass
Over memory's wizard glass !
Now, 'mid Scotia's hills and dells,
BURNS, with HIGHLAND MARY, dwells !
Now, 'neath Gallia's sunset glow,
JULIA wanders with ROUSSEAU !
Lo ! along the banks of Tweed,
Rove a happy pair indeed !
Shall thy worth be e'er forgot,
Lovely bride of WALTER SCOTT ?
Darker visions gloom along,
But they shall not shade our song.

These are pictures of that bliss
Which brightens life's dull willderness :
Oh, long may such glad visions beam
Over earth's perturbed stream,
As the silver stars that light
The darkness of a winter's night !

XIII.

But we've wandered from our theme away ;
 Let us seek the scene again,
Where the gathered Brave and Beauteous pay
 Honors to the bridal twain.
Now the merry tamborine,
Now the giddy violin,
Now the trump and drum are blent
With many a festive instrument !
And, in crowds that gaily glance,
Onward speeds the circling dance !

See, with gay and graceful charm,
Beauty leans on Valor's arm,
Listening to the whispered words
Thrilling all her spirit's chords !

Oh, her heart is like a harp,
  Where the hand of love might play!
Were it ever thus in tune,
  It would pour sweet songs alway!
Now, as circling round they go,
Floating on with music's flow,
On her fond, uplifted face,
Glows the famed Madonna's grace!
And the youth beside her moving,
Whither are his visions roving?—
He is gazing in her eyes,
  Far down in their fountains deep,—
Blue and bright as Autumn skies,
  Where the nestling Cupids sleep!
Ah, bold gazer, heed thee well!—
That is woman's chiefest spell!
Heed!—or she will bind thy heart,
As Cleopatra, by her art,
The Roman chief, though stern and brave,
Brought to her feet, a very slave!—
On with the dance,—nor gaze too long,—
That strain is Hope's delusive song!

XIV.

The dance goes on : to merry measure,
Light hearts speed the hours of pleasure.
Oh, how many shapes are here,
That shine in beauty's loftiest sphere !
And what charms of form and mien
Shed their witchery o'er the scene !
Never have mine eyes beheld
A scene of bliss that, this, excelled !

XV.

I do remember me that once,
  In Venice, on a night in June,
I mingled in the whirling dance
  Within a proudly-decked saloon.
Its sculptured walls were famed in story ;
  Around me wandered forms as bright
As Raphael's pencil wed to glory,—
  Embodiments of rosy light !
The scene was witchery !—and yet
  My heart, in sadness, turned away ;
It could not, in that trance, forget
  Bright forms beyond the western sea !

Those forms are wandering round me now,
  Are mingling in a sweeter dance ;
Kindness is writ on every brow ;
  Ah, is not this a deeper trance ?

XVI.

But soft !—amid the sparkling train,
Where youth and grace and beauty reign,
Who is she that meets the sight,
Like a "Phantom of Delight ?"
Though the forms around are fair,
None with her can now compare ;
Brightest planet in the sky !
Lodestar of each wondering eye !

XVII.

Sweet lady fair !—I need not tell
Thy gentle name : I own thy spell !
Throughout that glad and festal day,
Votive homage did I pay.
I stood beside thee in the dance ;
I watched thy blue-eye's ev'ry glance ;

I saw thy form glide graceful on,
As o'er the wave, Cayster's swan ;
I listened to thy playful words,
Sweet as the music of young birds ;
And, as I gazed, I felt my heart,
That long in joy had known no part,—
Around whose feelings time had thrown
A coldness like the winter stone,—
Melt into bliss beneath thy smile,
And gush with joy and love the while,—
As from the rock the fountains broke
Beneath the words the prophet spoke !—
And when the giddy dance was done,
  We wandered on the Steamer's deck,
And there, beneath the setting sun,
  While glowed the West with sheets of flame,
  And from the shore the soft wind came,
Lifting the curls upon thy neck,
I strove in vain my love to speak !—
Ah, little deem'dst thou at that hour,
What feelings in my breast had power !—
Could I have coined them into song,
Some strain, like this, had swept along :

XVIII.

LOVE'S METAPHORS.

Thou art a star, lady, thou art a star!
Gleaming in beauty and light from afar!
Heaven's own lustre shines in thy face,
And shrines thee in softness, virtue and grace:
  And many a heart, and many a knee,
  Lady, are bowing unto thee!
They throb, they beat, they sigh, they yearn,
For one glance of those eyes on them to turn!
  Those eyes,—those eyes,—those starry eyes!
  Cynosures worshipped by weak and wise!
As Chaldean shepherds worshipped, of old,
The stars they deemed Gods, and died to behold!
Though many they are, who thus bend at thy feet,
And would win thee, thou star, from thy blest retreat!
  Yet none of them love thee half so true,
  As the humble bard who now singeth for you!
Then deign, oh deign, on my path to shine,
Bright star of my worship!—blest, pure, and divine!

Thou art a rose, lady, thou art a rose !
Fragrant and lovely as any that blows !—
Though many a rival is round thee seen,
None, there are none, like the garden's queen !
  The lily is fair, but her cheek is pale,
  And looks the maid of some love-lorn tale ;
The violet's sweet, and the marigold,—
By none but the rose can thy lips be told !
  Those lips,—those lips,—those rosy lips !
  Flowers, where the honey-bee faints as he sips !
Ah, many a lover would die if he might
But press, for one second, those lips of light !—
Or hear them in kindness fragrantly breathe
The thoughts which he prays, may cluster beneath !
  Yes though there are such, none love thee so true
  As the humble bard who now singeth for you !—
Then deign, oh deign on my path to beam,
Sweet rose of my heart !—hope's Endymion dream !

Thou art a lute, lady, thou art a lute !
Whose strain of melody never is mute !
Never, oh never did bard repeat
His song of love in music more sweet,

Nor angel breathe his favorite hymn,
With richer tones 'mid the seraphim,
Than those that enrapturing float 'round thy way,
When thy heart and voice unite in some lay !—
That voice,—that voice,—that lute-like voice!—
Whose gentlest thrill makes the heart rejoice !
How many have hung entranced to hear
Its swan-like cadence fall on the ear !—
And many, now bowing around thee, deem
That thou art all music,—some heavenly dream !
Though many there be, none love thee so true
As the humble bard who now singeth for you !
Then deign, oh deign, to shed o'er his woes,
Light, music, and fragrance,—star, lute, and rose !

XIX.

Our gallant Steamer now had gained
The limits of her western way,
And proudly paused awhile to view
The glorious scene that round us lay !
Stained by the colors of the sunset sky,
A road of gold, the river rippled by ;

Far as the eye could reach, it gleamed away,
Beneath the flashes of the dying day ;
While, in the distance, like some Indian's boat,
Dim hurrying shadows o'er the surface float ;
Until, far reaching 'neath the sunset's pyre,
The rippling waters seem to melt in fire !—
 Oh, what a bright emblazonry,
 That evening, robed the Western sky !—
 Though ever in our gorgeous clime,
 It is a most impassioned time,
 And nobler pageants meet the eye,
 Than ever blazed in Italy,—
 Flinging Apollo's parting rays
 Above his earlier dwelling-place,
 As though the God still loved to view
 The shrines which once, his worship knew !—
 Or ever flashed o'er Sunium's steep,
 Turning to gold the Ægean deep,—
 As on that eve, when, through her isles,
 Ulysses fled Calypso's wiles,—
 And sky and wave and island bower
 Partook the passion of the hour !—
 Yet never was a lovelier even
 To raptured eyes, in beauty, given,

Beneath our soft, Ausonian heaven !
Where, proudly down, his journey done,
Had sunk, in pomp, the imperial sun,
An armament of clouds was seen,
With every gorgeous color, sheen ;
And now, above his kindling rays,
Their host is all one mighty blaze,
And, like a city wrapt in fire,
With wreaths of flame 'round every spire,
It glows before the gazer's eye,—
The blazing Moscow of the sky !

XX.

How lovely too, the scene around !—
'Tis rich traditionary ground.
Yon beetling cliff, so rugged, steep,
The Red Man called THE LOVER'S LEAP.
So high its top you scarcely now
Can mark the cedars on its brow ;
And the small streams, that, from it, come,
Are midway lost in rain and foam !—
And yet in olden times,—they say,—
A chieftain, from his foes, one day,

In triumph bore his bride away:
A hundred warriors quick pursued,—
A hundred warriors bent on blood!—
They track him through the devious wood;
At every turn they hem his path,—
Shouting with dread, relentless, wrath!—
On! fearless Rover of the wild,—
On! with thy foeman's treasured child.
Though ever swiftest in the chase,
'Tis now a fiercer, deadlier race.
On! with thy bride, nor pause for breath,
Thy only chance, escape, or death!
At length, in safety, with his bride,
He gains the river's anxious side;
But what a deadlier doom is this!—
They stand upon a precipice!
Upon its dizzy verge, they stand,—
Their coming foes on every hand!
One moment now they pause to hear,—
The vengeful warhoop echoes near!
There's no escape!—Shall that fair child,
By heartless fury be defiled?
Shall that young warrior, for *her* sake,
Die by the faggot and the stake?—

There's no escape ! Yes, heavens !— they leap
From off the summit of the steep !

Pale gazer on yon lofty cliff,
Tell me the fate of that bold chief !
Think you, that leap, he could survive,
And with the waves successful strive ?—
Ah, yes in safety o'er the tide,
He proudly bore his hard-won bride !—
And long his deeds shall live in fame,—
For TUSCALOOSA was that warrior's name !

XXI.

But now the scenes around grow dimmer :
The cliff and sunset fade away :
Soft through the skies the cold stars glimmer :
The young moon sheds her virgin ray.
Up with the steam !—our gallant vessel
Too long hath lingered on her way,—
Yet, ere we leave, one parting volley
The soldiers to their memories pay,
Whose names have shed a halo round the scene,—
The chief of this broad realm, and his wild forest-queen !

Hark, from the cliff, what echoes thunder !
The opposing banks reply in wonder :
The wild deer startled from his sleep,
Dashes along the lofty steep :
The eagle screaming soars around,
Scared by the rude, unwelcome sound.
Such sounds those hills have never heard,—
By such their quietude been stirred,—
Since famed De Soto, that wild Spanish rover,
With his fierce band, this gentle stream crossed
over !

XXII.

Now, up the stream, our graceful steamer
Speeds like a breathing thing along,—
While, in her cabin, many a dreamer
Listens to Beauty's witching song !
In festive mirth, dance on the hours,—
All hearts are wreathed with hope and bliss ;
And some,—the sterner sex,—in showers !—
Partake the goblet's beaded kiss !
Ah, bright Champagne !—the golden nectar,
The elixir fit for realms divine !—

Not Hebé, in her dalliance, decked her
  Goblets, with brighter waves than thine !
'Tis said,—and I believe the story,—
  That Bacchus, when he rose from earth,
Left, as memento of his glory,
  Thy recipé,—sweet source of mirth !
Ah, long may thy glad vintage brighten,—
  Impulse of pleasure and of song !
All sorrows of the heart to lighten,—
  Thy glorious waters sparkle long !
And oh, should wrinkled care o'ertake me,
  My purse give out,—my lady-love,—
As women will !—coldly forsake me,—
  No flowers around, no star above ;
Oh, then, my friends,—if I may ask it,—
  For doubtful 'tis if one remain,—
Send me in love—a half-a-basket
  Of Sillery's best star-champagne !

XXIII.

In mirth, we said, flew on the hours,—
In mirth and song in Beauty's bowers,—

If bowers the dreaming Muse may call
That Steamer's decorated hall !—
But ah, the bard cannot rehearse
Those mysteries in his fading verse :
How many hearts, that night, were won,
Or, sadder fate, were "quite undone !"
These sacred incidents, alone,
To such as felt them, can be known !
The whispered speech, the smothered sigh,
The tear-gem in the drooping eye,
The blushes o'er the bended neck,
The vows upon the strolling deck,
The frowns upon the Moon, whose light,
By lovers loved, was all too bright
For some that strolled that festal night,
Must all in secret live or die,
Unechoed by our minstrelsy !
Suffice it now in song to tell,—
The last notes of the sinking shell,—
That "all went merry as a *married belle!*"
And when at length our gallant barque
  Had gained her anchorage in the port,
And, slowly strolling through the dark,
  The scattered wanderers home resort,—

All hearts were brimmed with happiness,
In memory of the recent bliss,
And all with feeling's deepest swell,
Breathed forth,—or *should have breathed,* this fond

FAREWELL:

1.

Farewell ! to the Barque, that has borne us to-day,
In happiness, over the rolling wave ;
Oh, long, on the stream, may her bright pennons play,
Endeared to the hearts of the Fair and Brave !
And back when we turn from the shadows of time,
To gaze on the stars that brightened youth's sky,
The hours we past,
In her bosom, will last,—
The brightest and best, on the age-faded eye !

2.

Farewell, to the Bride !—who, in life's rosy hour,
Hath launched her frail shallop upon the sea ;
With innocence, beauty and love for her dower
And visions as gay as dream-poesy !

May prospering breezes, aye, fill her fair sails,
  And shadows her blue sky hever o'erwhelm,
      But brightly her boat
      O'er the deep waters float,
  With Hope at the prow, and with Love at the helm!

3.

Farewell to the Bridegroom!—the honored, the blest!—
  His sky is now lit by life's loveliest star!—
Oh, long be his heart with such pleasures possess'd,
  And never be shadowed by sorrow or care!—
His harp that, in sweetness, oft trembled with song,
  Oh, soon gush its fount with lovelier strains;
      And ever its strings,—
      As the dying swan sings,—
  Pour the gladdest of music while life remains!

4.

Farewell unto all, who have wandered to-day!—
  The brave and the lovely, the dull and glad,
The hearts that were swimming with visions all gay,—
  The heads that were swimming with *what they had had!*
To each and to all, a happy good-night!—

The hour is growing, for song, rather late :
But now as we part,
Oh, long, in each heart,
The memory live of the Nuptial Fete !

THE END.

www.ingramcontent.com/pod-product-compliance
Lightning Source LLC
LaVergne TN
LVHW010216110826
845151LV00004B/1107